MIDDLESEX
WITHIN LIVING MEMORY

WITHIN LIVING MEMORY SERIES

Other Counties in the series include:

Bedfordshire	Lincolnshire
Berkshire	Norfolk
Buckinghamshire	Northamptonshire
Cheshire	Nottinghamshire
Cumbria	Oxfordshire
Derbyshire	Shropshire
Dorset	Staffordshire
Essex	Suffolk
Gloucestershire	Surrey
Hampshire	East Sussex
Herefordshire	Warwickshire
Hertfordshire	West Midlands
Isle of Wight	Wiltshire
East Kent	Worcestershire
West Kent	North Yorkshire
Leicestershire & Rutland	West Yorkshire

MIDDLESEX
WITHIN LIVING MEMORY

Compiled by the Middlesex Federation
of Women's Institutes from contributions sent by
Institutes in the County

Published jointly by
Countryside Books, Newbury
and the MFWI, West Drayton

First published 1996
© Middlesex Federation of Women's Institutes 1996

COUNTRYSIDE BOOKS
3 Catherine Road
Newbury, Berkshire

ISBN 1 85306 425 4

Front cover photograph shows Manor Parade, Southall,
supplied by Maureen Handley, Harlington.
Back cover photograph shows Cole's smithy at Stanwell,
supplied by Beryl Wilkins, Stanwell.

Produced through MRM Associates Ltd., Reading
Printed by Woolnough Bookbinding Ltd, Irthlingborough

CONTENTS

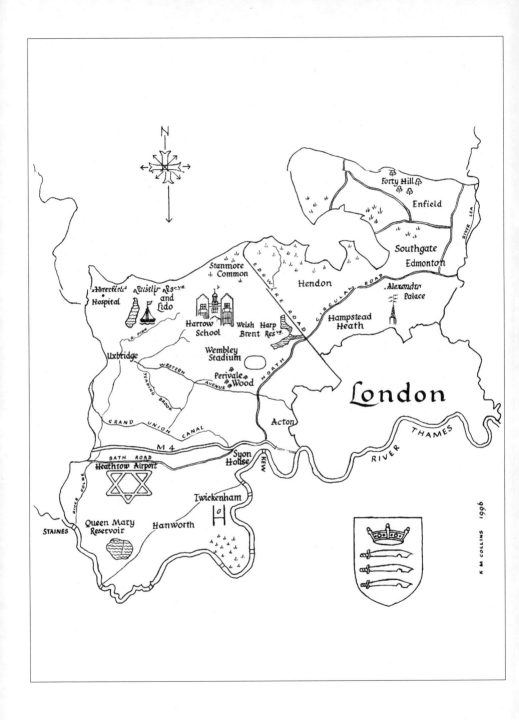

ACKNOWLEDGEMENTS

The Middlesex Federation of Women's Institutes would like to thank all members, their husbands, families and friends who supplied material and photographs for this book.

Unfortunately we were not able to include extracts from every submission. To do so would have meant duplication of content and of course, we had to take into account the space available. But all contributions, without exception, were of value in deciding the shape and content of the book. We are grateful for them all. My personal thanks to Hazel Dibbs of Hayes Town WI for typing the entries so efficiently, to Zeena Katrak of Northolt Afternoon WI for her clever interpretation of chapter headings in her beautiful line drawings and to Kathleen Collins of Ickenham WI for her superb map. We have all immensely enjoyed working on this book which marks our 75th anniversary.

Beryl Garrett
Co-ordinator

FOREWORD

The change from natural countryside to town takes many years and many people are involved in the changes – for better or worse. Since the beginning of the 20th century Middlesex has changed more than most counties and dramatically so after the development of Heathrow airport in the early Fifties which meant that large industrial estates, huge office blocks, hotels and row upon row of housing estates grew like mushrooms. These were followed by ribbons of new roads and motorways which covered areas where once trees stood tall in green meadows, surrounded by farmsteads and pretty cottages.

This does not mean that Middlesex has lost all its beauty. They have not yet managed to make a city here! Middlesex still has pretty villages with old pubs and village greens. It has parks, cricket clubs and bowling greens. It has Syon House, Osterley House, Hampton Court Palace and many lovely old manor houses across the county and there are lovely walks along the banks of the Thames. There are local history societies, museums, conservation groups, a Middlesex Society, and many WIs. These groups and others have done much during this century to help retain some of our green and pleasant land in Middlesex.

My thanks to all who have helped to make this book possible.

Beryl Garrett
Chairman

TOWN & COUNTRY LIFE

SOME TOWNS AND VILLAGES REMEMBERED

Green lanes where now juggernauts thunder by, horse-drawn carts and the sound of the blacksmith's hammer, small and family-run shops, cows driven along the road for milking – some memories of times which are not so long past.

❖ THE LOVELY VILLAGE OF ASHFORD ❖

'I was born in 1910 in Ashford which was then a lovely village – a mixture of large houses, farms, orchards, villas and cottages. In Feltham Road were the large houses where the Palmers and Ethel M. Dell lived with their attendant staff of maids, gardeners and coachmen. Facing them were orchards and cornfields, and the fruit being grown for a jam factory. Then came the Hearts of Oak, a typical country pub with a "jug and bottle" – almost like a large cupboard with a glass window which at the touch of a bell opened up to dispense the liquor. Then on to the village blacksmith known to all as Daddy Cooksey – a delightful old man who was everyone's friend and willing to perform all kinds of services, mending garden tools, giving advice on sick pets and despatching chickens for the faint-hearted.

There was the pond at the corner of Clock House Lane with willow trees, yellow iris and yellow water lilies, coots and ducks, which was a great attraction for children intent on collecting tadpoles and fishing for tiddlers to be taken home in a jam jar. Opposite this was the newly erected Roman Catholic church – an edifice of corrugated iron which after a fire some years later was replaced by a brick building. On the opposite side of the road was a farm and the King's Head, another ancient hostelry.

Next to the church was the Clock House Farm, a lovely black and white house with a thatched roof, where before it became a printing works, folk could take their jugs and buy milk.

Adjoining this was the Clock House – a really elegant building, with impressive door and balustrades along the top where peacocks were seen displaying. It had white wrought iron gates and railings and was flanked by a lodge and gardener's cottage and stable block. The clock from this building now stands in the recreation ground opposite.

The convent, formerly named Echelford House, had extensive grounds which ran between Feltham Road and Feltham Hill Road as far as Park Road. The Roman Catholic nuns took in girls rescued from the London streets and they were employed doing laundry work. They also ran a home for inebriated ladies, the wealthiest being accommodated in the large main house and others in the converted coach house which stood on the site of the present Roman Catholic school. Adjoining this was The Elms, another large house. On the corner of the Church Road was Muncaster School, a boarding school for boys, whose grounds covered Exeforde Avenue and today's Muncaster Estate. Opposite was another large house, Normanhurst. This was an impressive corner with many large trees complementing the grand old town tree with its iron seat and stone horse trough. This really was the centre of the village.

Of course, in those days horses were very much in evidence, Barleys, Butts and Dexters the bakers, all delivered bread every day by pony and trap and on Good Friday hot cross buns arrived on the doorstep about 7 am ready for the traditional breakfast. Milk floats came daily with their large churns and milk was ladled out. The various grocers in the village took orders and delivered goods by pony and trap. Meat and fish came by boys on trade bikes with large baskets on the front. "Fishy White" who traded from a private house collected his fish daily from a very early train from London and dispensed it from a three-wheeled contraption with a large box on the front containing ice.

The coalmen with their large carts and horses cannot be forgotten or the brewer's drays full of barrels and their shire horses, and the farm carts. All the horse traffic kept many a gardener busy with bucket and spade to help grow better crops.

In Feltham Hill Road were the Rowland Hill Almshouses and Ashford Lodge which had a long tree-lined avenue to the house and a long brick wall along School Road, also planted with pink flowered horse chestnut trees. A wonderful sight in the spring time. Along this road stood the Church of England school which was opened in 1860.

St Matthew's church was well attended in those days, the congregation being complemented on Sunday mornings by the pupils from the Welsh Girls' School, whose governors in 1882 had given money towards rebuilding the church.

In Church Road were situated several large houses where three doctors practised, the post office, and the county school which was then a fee paying school with a number of scholarships available to eleven year old children. In charge were Dr Knowles and Miss Pember, both strict disciplinarians. Adjacent and behind these buildings were Farmer Cook's fields which covered all the ground on which the houses in Village Way, Brownrigg Road, etc, now stand.

We had a large variety of high class shops and smaller ones, all privately owned where every need was catered for. There was a choral society, orchestral society, bowls, cricket and tennis clubs and all the churches had their own organisations. We also had a cinema where with great excitement we queued on Saturday afternoon for seats at about tuppence.

I started at Clarendon Road school at five years, where Miss George was headmistress and Miss Taylor, a lovely, gentle lady, was in charge of "infants". The highlight of the year was Empire Day when we were marched into the playground, where a small stage had been erected and the Union Jack was hoisted and patriotic songs were sung and poetry recited. Family and friends gathered outside the railings to watch.

During the 1914–1918 war many soldiers were billeted on homes in Ashford and stayed until they went off by train to France.

School holidays were spent walking, exploring lakes, footpaths and the river Ash, rich in wildlife and still with its stepping stones and the ford where the cart horses went through the water instead of over the old bridge. Quite a deep ditch ran along in front of the houses in Ford Bridge Road, protected by concrete posts – now railings. Swinging on this, of course, made a little diversion on our way to the river. Our pleasures were very simple but we had no time to get bored.'

▣ PRE-WAR CHISWICK ▣

'When I was a child before the Second World War, one could walk between Chiswick Southern railway station and Burlington Lane, via Sutton Court Road, or Park Road and Dukes Avenue, without let or hindrance. Now a six-lane highway, the Cromwell Road Extension, cuts Chiswick in half, and one side each of two roads, Cedars and Ellesmere, have vanished to make the road, the lifeline feeder to the M4. This road stretches between the notorious Hogarth Roundabout and the flyover.

As a child I remember that many of the beautiful houses, now no more, had their servants in cap and apron, answering the doors to errand boys: there were daily deliveries of bread, greengrocery and fish, and the milk roundsman with his horse even came on Sunday. No housewife had to go out to shop, and many houses had their tradesmen's entrances. The streets were blissfully clear of motor cars.

Until 1935 trams ran in Chiswick High Road and then the trolley buses were introduced. The 55 bus route provided transport to the High Road for one penny. I can remember the fare going up to 1½d. When the High Road was reached there were two department stores – Goodbans, a family firm, and a little upmarket Rankins (where Dillons bookshop now stands). If my mother was feeling rich she would go to Rankins for superior quality goods.

Early in the morning, sheep being driven into Caught's, the butcher, could be seen. A slaughterhouse was located beside the shop. At least the meat was fresh.

And, of course, a treat was to be taken to the Chiswick Empire to see the pantomime or the various famous comedians who topped the bill.

Chiswick was a delightful place to live in those days. The skies were clear; only beautiful birds inhabited our gardens. Now the magpie, jay and crow are our most frequent visitors, and Concorde thunders overhead. Can you wonder that the owls left us in the 1960s!'

◈ EASTCOTE MEMORIES ◈

'We became, in 1931, the proud owners of a house for a deposit of £50; the rates were about £10 the half-year, and the mortgage was £6 per month. The Northwood Electric Light Company supplied the electricity at the cost of 6½d and 1½d per unit. We could contract with the Pinner Gas Co (no Gas Board) for small coke for the boiler for 10s per month.

On the morning of our arrival Mr Robart the farmer had already left a sample pint of milk, and some cream. The opposite side of the road was just a field, and Mr Robart still had cows grazing there.

The shopping area was on the opposite side of the road. There was Apps the newsagent, Howard Roberts the grocer (cheddar cheese was 7d per ½lb), McKay the greengrocer (potatoes 7lb for 6d), Wilton the baker (large loaf 4½d, small loaf 2½d), Mr Stephen the fishmonger who would send up a fillet of plaice for 1s for the baby, Fox & Stride the iron-monger, a butcher, Mr Robart had a dairy shop, and Mr Johnson was both chemist and postmaster (by the pillar box).

There was a tennis court alongside the shops, and a hall which could be hired for dances, and it served as a cinema Wednesday and Saturday evenings. The price of seats was 9d, and 1s 3d for the best seat. There were often breakdowns with the films, and there were plenty of catcalls and wolf whistles. In Eastcote village there was another branch of Howard Roberts' which had a sub-post office, a butcher and a greengrocer, and a real country sweet shop (Mrs Tapping). On the opposite side of the road there was a forge, and it was the children's delight to watch the horses being shod. We still had the hunt here, and one often saw the riders go by in their pink coats. We had a haystack at the corner of Deane Croft Road and the Methodists used to bring out their portable organ on Sunday evening and give us their "songs of praise" by the side of the haystack.

It was still the old Metropolitan railway at the time we came here, and on a Wednesday and Sunday you could get a cheap return to Ealing for 7d, and a cheap return to Baker Street for 1s 2d. Eastcote station was only a rough wooden construction with plenty of holes, and it was nothing to see a rat poke its nose out of a hole and scamper around while you were waiting for a train.

Eastcote at that time was a great place for Sunday school treats (down by the Pavilion) and train loads of children used to come down on a Saturday afternoon in the summer months.

We still had the aristocracy living here. There was Lady Anderson whose house was where the Georgian flats now are, and it was a wonderful sight to see her lawn covered in crocuses in the spring. We also had Lady Warrender who lived at Highgrove and our local park is named after her.'

'When I arrived in Eastcote in 1945 it was still just a small village. There were no houses beyond Woodland Road, and Field End Road was a country road with hedgerows either side. There were small grocer's shops, including a small but very useful Sainsbury's, and all the stores would deliver groceries. In Old Eastcote was a smithy where my small boys used to watch the horses being shod.'

'My family moved to Eastcote from a small market town in Somerset late in 1945. It seemed to me, as a young person, that we had moved to the Metropolis, the contrast was so great. In fact, Eastcote was a partially developed suburb, as the outbreak of the war had halted the plans. Green fields were in evidence then, soon to be lost to many housing projects.

My most vivid memories of those days are quite mundane, but still alive within me. The shops were of that time. A small chemist/sub-post office appeared to be the hub of activity, and behind the post office counter sat the formidable sister of the pharmacist, like a galleon in full sail, frightening the potential purchasers of twopenny stamps.

A little way up the street from the chemist was the local cinema, known as the bug house or flea pit, a one storey, dismal building. Patrons endured a very uncomfortable time on the seats which rocked and rolled every time they were vacated or sat upon, and, yes – we did scratch ourselves occasionally.

Across the road was a divided shop, the one half of which was a lending library, run by a Joyce Grenfell look-alike who became very twee when teasing customers asked, "Have you any dirty books?" "No such thing in here," she would trill.

Traffic was almost non-existent. Early in the morning well dressed gentlemen walked over the crossroads, swinging their rolled umbrellas on the way to the Underground station and their power-bases in the city.'

'We moved to Eastcote in a flurry of snow in January 1965, to a bungalow looking across the Field End Road to a gateway into the grounds of Eastcote Place. Lady Anderson's grounds, we discovered, were thickly planted with daffodil bulbs in great banks on either side of the driveway, but by the next year the daffodils had all gone and instead, fronting onto the road, was the large block of flats named Georgian Lodge. When we had bought our bungalow Eastcote House was there in the middle distance, white and serene. "Don't worry to walk there now," we were told. By the time we moved in a few months later it had gone!'

◼ THE OUTSKIRTS OF LONDON PRE 1914 ◼

'How enormously things have changed since those pre-First World War days!

We lived in a four-storey house with a basement, on the outskirts of London in Middlesex. Coal was kept in the basement, being shot down a round hole in the pavement outside, into our cellar below. Everything was sent by horse-drawn carts to supply the houses and open coal-carts with strong shire horses paraded the streets at all times of the day, the man's raucous voice calling "Coal" for all who required it. Everyone burned coal for heating and cooking and the result was the awful yellow fog of Victorian times, the "pea-soupers" which descended on winter days. One really could get lost because the visibility would be only a yard or two. Coughs and colds resulted from breathing this fog and we muffled ourselves with scarves across our faces if we were obliged to go out in it.

Tradesmen called for orders early and had to get back in time for meat to be cooked for lunch. The light two-wheeled butcher's cart drove very fast with a high-stepping pony.

The houses were very cold in winter and as children we wore layers of clothes. A woollen vest went under a pair of combinations, then a liberty bodice to which were attached by buttons a pair of flannel knickers and then frilly cotton ones. A petticoat (flannel in winter) went under the dress. No wonder we looked so bunchy in early photos!

We had to make most of our own entertainment. Mother and father played and sang and friends came in for a musical evening on the pianola. One friend brought a gramophone. This had a large horn on the top for the sound to emerge. It had to be wound up with a handle on the side. I was five years old and fascinated by it. The band was playing out but I could not imagine how it got inside the horn!

A usual sight in the streets was a barrel-organ. This was like a piano on wheels. A man wound the handle whilst another went round and collected pennies. Poor children adored it and danced beside it on the pavement in spite of broken-down shoes.

All the houses in our street employed maids and also a woman came to us on Mondays to help with the washing. This was a big affair; a fire being lit early under the copper and baths full of blue water for the white things and one of starch for collars and cuffs, tablecloths etc., were placed ready. Oh, the steam everywhere, particularly on wet days when the washing had to be dried indoors! Then on Tuesdays the ironing was done (no drip-dry then). The frills on pillowslips, pinafores and aprons made extra work but looked very pretty.

Ladies, of course, had long skirts which just touched the

ground. These were edged with heavy braid to take the wear. Their long hair was piled up and kept in place with many hairpins. A matching arrangement called a "mouse" could be placed on the head and covered by the hair so that the style appeared more luxuriant. Hats were very large.

On Sundays everyone went to church in the morning and best new clothes were worn. Hats of course! One never went out without hats and gloves. My father wore a top hat to go to church or to business. The silk hat was brushed every morning and occasionally ironed with a special curved iron.

The greeting of all one's friends and neighbours outside the church after the service was always a social occasion. I also vividly remember the walk home with smells of succulent roasts issuing from the houses. In the afternoon, the bell of the muffin man was heard and we would often stop him and buy muffins for tea.

We were taken on shopping expeditions to Haringay or to Wood Green complete with pram or pushchair. The Penny Bazaar was the highlight of these trips because our weekly penny pocket money could be spent there. The Penny Bazaar was, of course, the fore-runner of Marks and Spencer and it was amazing the number of things that could be purchased for a penny; from little toys, sweets, cotton reels to useful articles such as needles and kitchen utensils.

I was nearly six years old when the first rumblings of war began. A family of Belgians moved into our road. They had a girl my age and I was shocked when she told me that they had to run away because the sky was red with burning houses! This was the first inkling a child had of the meaning of war.'

▣ THE HAYES GARDEN VILLAGE RAILWAY ESTATE ▣
'After the First World War the Great Western Railway had difficulty finding staff to man their big London terminus at Paddington because of the vast amount of factories in the surrounding area so they decided to bring people in from outside depressed areas, but these people would need houses to

live in and these were in very short supply. Together with the Welsh Building Society, who provided the mortgage, they decided to build their own houses on picturesque estates. These were to be managed by a board made up from the directors of the two companies and an equal number of tenants, all of whom together with paying rent would have to take out shares in the estates, thereby having a personal interest in their upkeep. So the two estates appeared, one at Hayes, Middlesex and the other at Acton. Every neighbouring semi-detached house had to be built to a different design with a plot of garden surrounding it. Also every street had to be well lighted and tree-lined with flower plantations spotted along them.

The first houses to be built in 1923 at Hayes were in Minet Drive, named after the person that the land originally belonged to. Then followed Hunters Grove, Crossways, East and West Walks, Minet Gardens, Halsway, Cherry Grove and Showers Way. In 1935 Birchway appeared; this road was built in three sections and the first street party enjoyed by the children of the whole road was for the coronation of George VI and Queen Elizabeth, the now Queen Mother. After this Halsend was built, followed by Herman's Grove. The bottom end of Minet Drive was in progress just before the Second World War started and all building had to cease. Because of this only one side of the street was completed and it remained an unmade-up road until after 1986. The foundations of the new road which had been laid north of Birchway never were completed and after the war this land was taken over by the council to build the Avondale Estate.

The agreement was that every tenant on the estates had to work for the Great Western Railway and people came from all over the South Western area of England and from South Wales to live in these houses, enjoying homes the like of which they had never been used to before – three bedrooms, built-in range for cooking with back-boilers which also gave constant hot water (the pipes from the boiler often ran across the lounge ceiling to an upstairs airing cupboard providing a form of central heating never experienced before), plus everyone had an inside toilet and bathroom, what bliss! Also, of course, they had new jobs to come to. Over 600 houses were finally built in Hayes alone. After the nationalisation of the railways in 1948 only employees of British Rail who worked on the Western Region anywhere in the country were allowed to take out a tenancy on the estate. In 1984 after, I understand, the owners of the Welsh Building Society had all ceased to exist and the charity trust set up by the Great Western Railway Company to protect the tenants could be broken by law, the estates were sold to their present tenants and so the Hayes Garden Village Tenants' Association ceased to exist.'

◈ A DRIVE IN HAYES TOWN ◈

'On a lovely summer evening we drove along the Dawley Wall in Hayes Town. We passed Billy Benn's farm on the right, on the left we came to Rigby Cottages, all with dry toilets which the council came and emptied every week. We drove up the lane until we came to the Whitehouse pub, a lovely country retreat, very basic inside but you could sit outside in the garden and have a drink. Jack George, the owner, would chat to us and tell us of his experiences. He drove a bull-nose Morris Cowley; the battery was on the running board, on the other side was the spare wheel. The locals used this pub. One chap used to say about 10 pm when you got hungry, "I will be over the field in the morning and get a bag of mushrooms, cook them for breakfast with a slice of gammon."

We could walk along by the canal and come out at the bottom of Hayes Bridge. It was a small bridge then, not as big as Bournes Bridge of today. There was a row of cottages at the side and the local policeman lived there. He ruled Hayes Town with a rod of iron. Children saw him coming and fled.'

◈ SUNBURY ON THAMES IN 1929 AND 1956 ◈

'I came to live at Sunbury on Thames in 1929, at the age of 13 years. At that time, the only transport was a train to Waterloo every half hour. Very few people owned a motor car and the only other form of transport was a bicycle. For any entertainment or to do any shopping outside Sunbury, apart from the train, one had to ride or walk at least five miles. Strangely though, in those days, Sunbury Common had four good grocery shops, three butchers, dairies, bakers, haberdashers, hardware suppliers, a shoe shop and cobbler – in fact, we were almost self-contained as far as living was concerned and everything was brought to the door, this with a population of approximately 3,000 people.

In 1929 Sunbury Common, as it was then called, was a rural area, devoted mainly to orchards and nurseries growing flowers, salad crops and fruit for the London markets. Green Lane where I lived was surrounded by a field, a market garden and a chicken farm. Behind our house, which was one of about twelve in the lane, was a lake of some extent, an ex-gravel pit, fished regularly by anglers from as far afield as London and in which we were able to swim. After the war, the lake was infilled with debris from the bombed area of London and houses built on the farm and the field. The infilled area finally had its quota of housing.'

'When we first moved to Sunbury the nearest grocer traded under the name of "Good". He had a wonderful shop, quite small in front but with storage space behind. The counter was made of deep rich mahogany, with brass scales gleaming, and most of the dry goods were weighed out while you waited into blue bags of sugar paper. There was a delivery service, one put in one's order and it was brought right into the kitchen. I made my own bread regularly and had to send away to Sussex for stone-ground wholemeal flour. It came by post in 14 lb hessian sacks, which one returned. Sometimes my husband would come in from work and ask if there was any kneading to be done. If there

was he would volunteer and rid himself of the frustrations of the day!

As I always had a washing machine (my mother had had one in 1937 so I was brought up with them) I did not use a laundry service, but there was one in Sunbury which prided itself on being an "open air" laundry and used to hang all the washing on lines in the area which is now a business estate.

A grocer was working locally until he was well over 90 years old. He used to cook hams on the bone and hand slice them extremely finely. He must have started work at around the turn of the century or earlier, at the age of twelve years, and used to walk every week from Sunbury to Richmond through orchards all the way. Now it is very built up.

The British Petroleum Research Centre was quite small in 1956, and a lot of the land covered by some of its buildings was previously farm and market garden land and then being dug up for gravel. BP had a hooter which sounded every Friday at noon; it was so loud that I had to stand by the pram to calm the baby. In those days one automatically put the baby into the pram and left it in the garden to sleep or watch the leaves of the trees waving in the breeze. With the cat net or the insect net in place one had no doubt but that the child would be safe.

The nearest thing we had to a play group was the baby clinic, where there were a few large toys and the mums could sit and chat. We were very lucky to have a nursery class in the local infants' school, but competition was very keen to secure a place. The class was a remnant of the wartime day nursery and took the children all day from the age of four years. The child's name had to be registered soon after birth to obtain a place, which was hard for those moving into the district. In 1964, when our third child was three years old, some friends and I got together, all having children of a similar age who seemed to need some extra stimulation, and we started a playscheme. One mother would take all five children into her home for one morning a week and devote that time to playing with the group. It worked extremely well and all the children benefited enormously.'

◙ STANWELL IN THE 1930s ◙

'I was born in Isleworth and have lived in Middlesex all my life – how things have changed in 60 years! My grandmother's house was situated in Long Lane, between Ashford and Stanwell, and she used to run a small Women's Mission somewhere in that area.

This was called the Band of Good Hope and after the Second World War – when I believe the hall was bombed – she ran it from her own home in Stanwell Road where she had then moved.

My grandmother was a keen gardener and very fond of the great outdoors. I can well remember her taking us for walks through miles (it seemed miles to me at the age of four) of open countryside on hot summer days – the fields full of poppies and cornflowers, humming bees and insects, in and around Stanwell! Now, alas, all those beautiful fields have gone and are replaced by the buildings of Ashford Hospital, enormous housing estates, oil depots and Heathrow Airport. The reservoirs had just been constructed and they in turn provided more interesting walks for all weathers. Happily there are still footpaths across these vast expanses of water, providing a sanctuary for an enormous quantity of wildfowl.'

◙ A RABBIT BY POST ◙

'In the 1930s there were three postal deliveries in Middlesex, London and surrounding counties. My grandfather who had a farm just over the border in Buckinghamshire would often send a rabbit by early post, with feet tied and a piece of brown paper wrapped round the middle with label attached, and we would receive it safely by the afternoon post. A few of the first snowdrops were always put in an envelope early morning and received by afternoon.'

◙ NORTHOLT IN THE 1930s ◙

'I was born in Church Lane (now Church Road), Northolt in

1931. There were only a few houses in the lane then and some more down in the village near St Mary's church. There was a field of cows next to our house. The hub of the village was Raven's shop which sold nearly everything including oil and it had its own bakehouse. I can remember the smell of the shop – a mixture of oil and groceries.

Other shopping was done in Greenford. We thought nothing of walking the two miles because there was no public transport. When any major item was needed we went to West Ealing on the "pull and push" train from Northolt Halt. I would be given a penny to put in the Nestlé's chocolate machine on the platform. It was an all day expedition and would include lunch at Lyons Teashop where we usually had steak and kidney pie followed by a cream bun.

The pony racing at Northolt Park provided a lot of trade for the area as the jockeys and trainers used to lodge in pubs and local houses when race meetings were on. I am told that some of my first words were, "They're off!" from my vantage point on my father's shoulders.'

▣ THE LAMPLIGHTER AND THE MUFFIN MAN ▣

'In 1933/34 when Bishop Ken Road was completed in Sudbury, the street lamps were electric. The local council must have decided that these were expensive, as they were suddenly changed to gas.

At dusk a lamplighter rode around on his bicycle carrying a ladder. He stopped at each lamp, propped his ladder against the projecting arm, on the lamp, climbed up and lit the lamp, repairing it with a new mantle when necessary. This ensured that lamps were never out of action for more than one evening. The lamplighter must have returned at sunrise to extinguish them, but I do not recall seeing him.

All lamps were extinguished during the war. After the war, with increasing traffic, higher lamps were needed to illuminate the road – electric lamps were then installed, needing higher, mobile equipment to see to them when they failed.

In winter the muffin man was familiar on the streets. About

four o'clock he would come by, ringing his bell, his hot muffins carried, under a cover, on a board on his head. Costermongers used to bring round their drays with vegetables, announcing their arrival with a bell, and using acetylene lamps in winter time to show up their wares.

Heavy cart horses sometimes deposited a free mass of manure in the road which residents quickly scooped up for additional fertiliser on their gardens.'

Standing on the frozen Thames at Pharoahs Island in 1954.

Ferry Lane, Pharoahs Island during the floods of 1947.

🔹 FIFTY YEARS ON PHAROAHS ISLAND 🔹

'I moved to Pharoahs Island in April 1941. The island did not have water laid on – we had to row to the ferry point on the tow path to get drinking water and we pumped river water in for all other uses; all the bungalows had cess pits. Water was the first to be installed on the island, main drainage came a long time afterwards. Very few homes even had a telephone in those days; it was war time, there were no motor boats on the river and very few cars on the tow path.

During the very bad floods of 1947 we rowed our boat from the front door to Church Square, the first dry ground for us. Children were unable to go to school for two weeks, but were then evacuated by army DUKS and stayed with friends in the village. When the water went down it left a terrible mess, everything was covered in thick mud. About a week after we returned to our home there was a terrible smell near the fireplace in the lounge; when the floor boards were taken up a dead rat was discovered which had become wedged under the bungalow during the flood.

Some time after the floods we were grateful to receive food parcels from Shepparton, Australia; they contained tinned fruit which even in 1947 was still very scarce. Another memorable winter was 1962 when the river froze over completely, it was hard enough to drive cars upon. One morning as I walked across on my way to work I slipped and sprained my ankle. A rope had been put across which we walked along just in case the ice cracked.

The island is a very different place now. In 1941 only about half the bungalows were lived in, they were considered as holiday homes pre-war but as the years went by more residents stayed all the year round.'

◙ MEMORIES OF SHEPPERTON ◙

'I lived at 168 Green Lane, Shepperton and started school at the church infants' school which was situated at the end of the High Street near the war memorial. My brother who was 18 months older than me went to the church school for the older children just a few yards away. We had to take packed lunches and I went up to the other school to have mine with my brother. As we got older it was felt we would get a better education at the council school which was at the end of Sheep Walk (at the other end of Shepperton which was known as Shepperton Green) and so my parents had us transferred to there. It was a long walk as there were no buses and I remember on one winter's morning the roads were like ice and so my mother put long woollen socks on over our boots and, holding each of our hands, walked us to school. My sister who was younger was left at home.

At the bottom of our garden were fields of hay and when it had been cut two or three children who lived near and we three would get through and make ourselves houses, and thoroughly enjoy our time out there. There was so much more freedom then.

There was hardly any traffic along Green Lane and there were ditches each side of the road in some parts. There was a concrete path outside our place and some of us would draw with chalk the necessary squares for hopscotch and play many a game.

The paper shop in the High Street was then James's who also sold sweets. He had what was called a halfpenny box which contained all sorts of childish delights such as sherbet dabs, sweet tobacco, gobstoppers, aniseed balls, etc. Each Saturday we three children would be given a penny which was our pocket money for the week and go down there to spend it. This was the highlight of the week. I remember one Saturday it was pouring with rain and rather than disappoint us our mother said she would go down and get what we wanted and so she was given a

The Anchor Hotel, Shepperton in a more leisurely age.

list – we each wanted different things and we waited in anticipation with my Dad in charge until she got back. She must have been a saint!

The house on the corner of Broadlands Avenue near the station was then the home of Dr Urquhart who was a very caring and good doctor. When I was twelve years old I had to have my appendix out in Walton Cottage Hospital. There was not a children's ward and my mother apparently was concerned that I would be with ladies discussing things that would not be good for a sensitive child! Our dear doctor, therefore, arranged for a small children's ward to be created to put her fears at rest. Such was his dedication.'

▧ Now So Changed ▧

'Memories can be a singular thing or a group thing. Ask older people what they remember about the death of George VI and they will tell you what they were doing – I was talking to the telephone operator of the manual exchange at Stanmore. Ask them what they were doing when Kennedy's death was announced and they will give you chapter and verse. I was driving through North Harrow.

But singular memories are usually brushed aside which is a shame as they give an insight into the world as it was. Memories of places now changed out of all recollection. I remember Honeypot Lane as a country lane where, when we drove down it in Father's car the hedgerow scratched the side of the car.

My mother remembers Burnt Oak without shops, just the new tube station and the United Dairies for groceries. When I was christened in 1930 my godfather couldn't turn his car round outside St Margaret's, Edgware, as the road was too narrow. Edgware as the graceful shopping area it used to be with the draper's Stanley J. Lee – where you had a chair to sit on when ordering your materials or buying your silk stockings; Nurseryland with its coach built prams; Gainsborough's the bookshop and stationers; Lawleys the beautiful china shop. Watling Avenue, Burnt Oak with its barrows lining the kerb selling fruit, vegetables and clothes. The fishmonger with the tray of live eels, the boy at the top of the road who sold lemons at six for 5d. The butchers who sold meat cheaply at five o'clock on a Saturday evening so as not to have to store it over the weekend.

All memories of a world now long gone and which will never return.'

◙ OUR WORLD IN 1916 ◙

'Our world in 1916, when I was seven, just involved Laleham, Staines, Ashford and Shepperton. It was very quiet and rural, no buses, walking everywhere or cycling. We loved the clean water where we swam, paddled and fished, making nets of old net curtains and wire.

There were two farms at Laleham, with those lovely horses ploughing the fields. A blacksmith came from the same family for generations.

Where the river Ash flowed under the bridge at Ashford was a lovely place to paddle. Every winter we took a walk to see the flooding of the Thames at Shepperton. There were steamers on the river in summer, and a regatta at Laleham every year on the 6th August, with a village brass band and always a fair in a field near the river. Barges went through the locks up the river to Staines, full up with coal for the Gas, Light & Coke Company.'

◙ GREENFORD ◙

'I came to live in Greenford in 1947. To me, it had the look of a seaside town, with its tidy streets and rows of neat houses. I would stand at the top of the Broadway and take pleasure in the line of orderly shops, and also in the view beyond the Broadway looking up towards Hanger Hill.

The Broadway had every type of shop one would ever need. We went to Rose's for hardware – no matter what you were looking for Mr Rose would have it somewhere! Other shops included Hawkins, Sydneys, Clarke's, Kirby the butcher, Woolworths with its high counters just out of reach of little fingers, Boots, Howards, Williams, Macfisheries, Myers for furniture, Lavells, and down the steps to the lively fruit and vegetable stall, with the banter of the assistants as they coaxed the passers-by to buy their bargains. They sometimes gave away a bag of fruit as goodwill. We had a couple of banks, two cinemas – the Granada and the Playhouse, Wards the jeweller's, a post office, two schools, the Red Lion pub, and so much more. There was a thriving covered market with stalls selling fresh fish, meat, greengrocery and anything else. Just down the hill we had our good old-fashioned cobbler, who would stitch anything. There was the 50 shilling tailor's, and just off the Broadway we had a police station, a health clinic and a library.

Often on summer afternoons we would walk along the country road, Ruislip Road, to Northolt aerodrome for a picnic and the children would play in the sandpit there. On Sunday afternoons we would either walk across to Bunny Park to talk to the rabbits, play ball, have an ice cream and walk back across the golf links, emerging in Dormers Well Lane to lean over the farm gate to give the horses an apple, or we would walk to Perivale and up Horsenden Hill. The hill was a must after the first snow. Personally, I would have stopped the clock at 1959.'

▣ ENFIELD IN THE FIRST WORLD WAR ▣

'We were one mile from the centre of Enfield through Baker Street which boasted many lovely old houses (gentlemen's houses) to the borders of Forty Hill. There was no public transport then, in the early 1920s.

Our house was a six double-roomed family house plus scullery with hearthstone copper, but no bathroom and an outside door to the toilet. Therefore the copper fire was constantly being lit, with the small penny bundles of chopped firewood (bought from the door to door salesman, who also sold paraffin for the lamps, and candles) to heat water for baths and the weekly wash. As children our baths were always in a portable tub in front of the kitchen range, so warm and cosy. The kitchen range was religiously blackleaded and the fender and fire irons of shining steel cleaned with emery paper. Much of the cooking was done in the oven of the range, with kettles of water heating on top.

Just around the corner was Percy Ansell's High Class Butcher's with its own abattoir, where we children would watch with bated breath when cattle for slaughter were unloaded, secretly hoping that one or two would escape when being guided through a narrow alleyway into Mr Ansell's field. It did happen quite often and it was like the Spanish Bull Run to us, screaming with excitement when the animals thundered past us hiding in our gardens.

Next to Ansell's was Bridge House, where Mr Greenall the bookmaker lived, then Mr Stiles, High Class Grocer, and the post office run by Miss Marshall and her sister. Then the village pond which always froze in winter for us to slide on, next to which stood the smithy. How we loved to watch the smith at work with his bellows to boost the blaze to make his horseshoes. I can still smell the scent of burning when he put those hot shoes on the horses' hooves and we wondered whether the horses could feel it, even though they stood so quietly.

There was the little cobbler, Mr Yellerby (Yellowbelly to us kids), "foreign" he was, we thought, and a row of cottages, "Cottage Row", housed workers from the estate of Forty Hall, home of Col Sir Henry Bowles, which was later inherited by his grandson, Derek Parker Bowles.

Over the bridge and up the hill we come to Myddleton House where E. Augustus Bowles, the legendary gardener and misogynist lived and where we had our Sunday school outings. Nearby lived Frances Perry, one of the 20th century's most notable figures in the world of horticulture, and a young protege of E. A. Bowles, who encouraged her in her early years. She helped found Capel Manor Institute of Horticulture nearby, now an Adult Training Centre. Frances Perry never retired and books flowed from her pen, but though she travelled in more than 70 countries, studying plants and lecturing, she spent most of her life at Enfield, "a village in rural Middlesex", which she saw engulfed by the sprawl of Greater London, as I too who have lived in Enfield all my life, have seen.'

◼ FROGGING ON STANWELL MOOR ◼

'Well, I have been about a bit but I have never met anybody else who used to go frogging like we did. Now, first, you get an old stocking, lisle if possible, tie a large knot at the toe end, then find a good stout stick, put on your wellies and away you go. Early morning is the best time. Stanwell Moor in those days, the 1930s, had lots of streams. You go along the banks of the stream hitting the bank just above the water line and out jump the frogs. Then you swoop down, grab the frog and put it in your stocking. On a good morning you could catch quite a few, take them home and put them in a wet sack, tie the top but quite often they escaped and caused mayhem. You must keep the sack wet so you dip it in the stream now and then. Once a week the frogman comes around on his bike to collect them. We were told they were used to feed rare snakes at London Zoo; he would loudly ring his bell and out would run all the children clutching a wet sack. The man would take the frogs out, if they were too small he would throw them back in the stream, if big enough he would pay you one penny for each frog, big business. I often wonder if there are any frogs at Stanwell Moor now, if so they must be of a very modern strain because I feel sure they must have been extinct before the war.'

◼ SOUTHALL FRAGMENTS ◼

'We had a butcher's shop in Southall in the early years of the century. My father used to go to Smithfield Show and buy the prize beast, have it brought to his own abattoir in Southall, slaughter it himself and arrange a huge display of the meat, complete with award cards and rosettes which covered the whole of the open fronted shop. This display remained for the whole of the week prior to Christmas. It was covered by a tarpaulin at night and watched over by a night watchman complete with brazier to keep him warm. On Christmas Eve the

S 15934   Town Hall, Southall

The Town Hall and Manor Parade, Southall between the wars.

Manor Parade, Southall.

meat was auctioned off by my father; there were no freezers in those days.

My other early memory is of the barge horses and bargees that worked the Grand Union Canal. The horses were stabled at the local gas works in White Street, Southall. They were collected by the bargees at 7 am and returned at 5 pm and as they passed by our shop one could always tell the time of day by their appearance. May I add that "Top Locks" was a favourite playing spot for us youngsters where we used to fearlessly run to and fro across the lock gates.

Oh for those happy days when children could safely disappear for the day with a bag of sandwiches and a "bottle of pop".'

'On the Norwood Green/Southall border is the famous Three Bridges. This consists of the Grand Union Canal running over the railway line, which ran from Brentford to Southall, and a road bridge crossing over the top of the aqueduct which carries the waters of the canal. Until recently, barges sailed along the canal, the "rubbish trains" ran at night between Brentford and Appledore, and, of course, traffic still goes over the road bridge. When I was a small child there were bluebell woods close by and my father took me to see the bridges when we were picnicking in the woods one day.'

◧ COWLEY AND ICKENHAM ◧

'I was born on 1st August 1915 on an extremely hot day, so I was told. While my mother was "labouring" with me my father was celebrating at the Fox Inn opposite. All around were cherry orchards, as we lived then in a three-storied house in Cowley with my grandparents.

One of my earliest memories was going to Ickenham in a horse-drawn pantechnicon with aunts and uncles. The ladies all wore their long hair piled high on their heads and beautiful big hats on top, and we spent the day picnicking in Swakeley House grounds; Swakeley Road was then called Back Lane and very bumpy.

In 1951 I moved to Ickenham, having had to wait until we had

A family picnic in the grounds of Swakeley House, Ickenham.

a large number of points and two children before we could buy a house. It was the last house in the road at that time and fields stretched up to Harvil Road, and the rabbits ran about and cows grazed there. One night we awoke to a lot of noise and the cows had moved down into our front garden which had been newly laid out – my husband's comments were unprintable!

Swakeley Road had just been built as a double carriageway and there were several accidents there when 30 mph was the limit for traffic.

Ickenham High School for Girls and Copthall Road Farm both disappeared and the present Eleanor Close and United Reformed church, Rectory Way were built, and a new St Giles' rectory, which took us up to two cottages and Gell Cottages, which were originally called "The Almshouses". The Buntings was a small cafe on the corner, then turned into a nursing home by the Abbeyfield Society, since moved to Court Road. It is now a solicitor's office.

The bus fare to Uxbridge and Ruislip was 2½d. The train station was a wooden halt with a gate and a slope each side down to the trains. Hillingdon station was a halt too, even worse for getting in and out.'

❖ SIPSON VILLAGE ❖

'I was born in the lovely village of Sipson, where my childhood was very happy and carefree. Everyone was our friend.

We were born in Holly House opposite to Mr Tomkins' shop, which is still there. He sold everything for everyone's needs; it was a wonder he found anything, but he did. Our house was where Vincents Close is now.

Mr and Mrs Gelpin lived at the Crown public house next to us. My mother and Mrs Gelpin joined Harmondsworth WI as there was not one in Sipson. When they were coming home one evening they thought it was a foreigner coming towards them. Mrs Gelpin jumped into the ditch and broke her arm. It was her son come home; he was in his uniform, he worked with Lord Baden-Powell with the Scout movement so wore a large hat and shorts so you can guess how he looked in the moonlight. They laughed afterwards, so did the village.

The other side of us was Miss Phillips who had a farm, we used to take a blue can with a lid on to get our milk. Talking of milk, there was a man that came round the village with big cans on a horse and cart. The cans had lovely shiny taps on, and one

day I turned them on and then went and told my mother there was white rain going down the drain. She was not very pleased as she had to pay for it.

We had lots of ground with Holly House. My mother used to get up at three o'clock in the morning to pick white and bluebells and lilies to be ready for the man to take to Covent Garden. Mr George Chandler was the driver who lived in Gladstone Terrace in the village. The big pear tree that was in our front garden was a help as my mother sold the pears to pay the rates.

The house belonged to Mr Whittington who lived at Trustlers Farm down Harmondsworth Lane. Mr Whittington wanted to come and live in our house as he wanted the bigger house and garden, so we were moved to a little cottage up the road. My mother said that was one of the times when she could have run away without putting her hat on. It was a big farmhouse made into four little cottages, and before very long we were all good friends.

This was the only thing I did not enjoy – we had a pump for the four houses. In the winter to melt the ice we had to pour boiling water down the pump before we could get any water. It was lovely water, although our teeth chattered. The Wiggins family always seemed to get there first.

In the summer holidays my mother used to take nearly all the children down to Harmondsworth Moor with our bottles of bright yellow lemonade powder. We spent the day paddling and catching tiddlers; the water was very clear and clean. The picnics were lovely, although I remember it was only bread and jam. My mother used to take a loaf and jar of jam, it tasted good with your friends. Of course, we always had to walk both ways but we used to sing hymns at the top of our voices, which helped us along the lane. We were all such good friends no one seemed to quarrel and they obeyed my mother.

I must mention the Ploughing Match. It was a red letter day in the village when most of the boys played truant, my brother amongst them.

In the evenings we all played together. We had a skipping rope right across the road; the two that were turning the rope used to put it down flat on the ground for the bicycles to go over and the odd car. There were only two cars in the village, belonging to Mr Wild and Mr Robbins, and, of course, there was Mrs Wild in her lovely pony and trap. We bought bicycles when we left school, from a man in Harmondsworth at the garage. One shilling a week, and mine cost a few shillings. Then we had the three Miss Hoods who lived in a lovely little house in the village called The Homestead. The ladies always rode their three-wheeled bicycles, which we tried to ride but failed, only had a good laugh. We did enjoy ourselves, so did they.

One day we were indoors having our dinner when we saw red hot coals falling down in our cupboard next to our fireplace, which was a very old fashioned grate. The fire engine was sent for and by that time all the village was outside; just to see a fire engine was a treat in those days. Anyway, someone suggested sending for Mr Howel who lived in 18 Row as he would remember how the chimney was altered, so down the road came Mr Howel. He had a lovely beard and all the children were following just like the Pied Piper, what a picture, try to imagine it. Of course, he knew the answer, there was a ledge that should have been filled in, so all was well. Afterwards my mother said, "Look, have one of my Sunday cakes, that will make you feel better." We believed her, you see we only had cakes on a Sunday. Off we went to school feeling very important.

Another time, I remember, our houses were struck by lightning. The little girl next door was taken ill. I can still see my mother going out to get a doctor with her nightie on, my Dad's wellington boots, his cap and overcoat, what a sight.

There was great excitement in the village when Miss Preston started the Girls' Life Brigade. We loved our uniforms, the night we were measured for them we swanked about. We paid for them weekly, one shilling a week.

For our Sunday school treat we all walked over to the canal at Yiewsley and went on a narrow boat to Harefield, had races in a field and tea. We thought it was abroad, it seemed so far away from Sipson. We came home tired but happy. We loved the horses that pulled the boat.

On Whit Sunday we always had a new straw hat with daisies

round the brim. Shoes, socks and dresses were bought from a lovely little shop by West Drayton Green belonging to Miss Swift. On Whit Monday we all walked down the lane to Mr Bateman's meadow for a wonderful day. I can remember we named the cake "Sunday School Cake". It was a lovely sight going down the lane as we had 200 children. When we got a little older we were allowed to help with the sandwiches in the tithe barn; I felt ten feet tall, which was a miracle as I was only four foot ten inches.

Another thing we did was to walk up to the Bath Road to see the "charas" come home from Ascot races. They used to throw pennies to us children. The first time I picked one up, I promptly fainted.

My dad was a sidesman for 31 years at Harmondsworth church. As the harvest was on we all went as we loved the singing; we sat at the back of the church with the bell ringers. It was a wet evening so my mother hung her umbrella on the back of her seat. When we came out it was still raining, up went the umbrella, out fell lots of little onions. My mother did not know what to do, so we all had a good laugh and went home happy. The bell ringers were to blame.

Most people worked for Wild and Robbins. Well, they had to because we all lived in their houses, and that was the rule. My dad earned 30 shillings on the land and our rent was four shillings. Less money but happier.

I remember Bridget Sullivan used to go to the King William for a jug of beer. When she saw us coming out of chapel she hid it under her apron. We always hoped she would drop it but she never did.

We had a toilet at the bottom of our garden. It had a wooden seat which my mother used to scrub. It backed onto next door, so we could talk to each other. My friend that lived next door and I made arrangements what time to meet down there. We used to take a candle, you shaded it with your hands, scared in case it went out, we still laugh about it.'

◘ OPEN AIR SERVICES ◘

'As a child in Hayes I was brought up in the Salvation Army and one of the things I loved the most, even after I left the Army, was the open air services. The band and songsters used to meet at the arranged places, form a circle, raise the flag, and that was their church. The band would play the hymns and the songsters would join in. They were always lively hymns such as *All things bright and beautiful* and *Fight the good fight*. People would come out of the houses and join in, or just to put money in the box, and stand on their doorsteps and listen. A member from the Salvation Army would read a passage from the Bible, and say a prayer. When the service ended, after only about half an hour, the band would form up behind the flag bearer, the songsters behind them and they would march off towards the Salvation Army hall. The music could be heard for many streets away. As they marched other people would form in behind and follow them to the hall. After this a full service would take place inside the hall.

This took place twice a day on Sundays in the summer, ten o'clock in the morning and six o'clock in the evening. The evening one was generally held on the spare ground outside Caswell & Pickups, the chemist. In the winter it was only held in the mornings.'

◼ RUISLIP IN 1950 ◼

'We came to live in Ruislip in 1950, on the corner of South Drive and Brickwall Lane.

There was a single decker bus which, presumably terminating its run, turned round on our corner, there being of course no bus station at Ruislip. Indeed, the approach to the Underground station was lined with little huts and shabby offices, mostly of coal merchants – Times House was built much later.

Another thing I remember was that our street lights went out late in the evening. One lady we knew opposite was most upset when they were to be on all night as she thought she wouldn't be able to sleep!

There were two cinemas, the Rivoli at the bottom of Ickenham Road, later Sainsbury's supermarket, and the Astoria in the High Street opposite the end of Brickwall Lane, so cars often parked all round our corner – much banging of car doors when they came out.

My husband got a car very soon for his business, which was a great excitement, but bicycles were the means of locomotion locally for me and the children. We soon acquired a dog and then I learnt all the beautiful walks, through the Manor Farm, to the Pinn Fields and Ruislip Woods and further afield when we took her on the bus to the Lido. I remember walking down through allotments where the Winston Churchill Hall now stands. And many happy hours were spent by my son and his friends fishing in the river Pinn with a jam jar for minnows.

The children attended the Bishop Winnington-Ingram School which was then in Eastcote Road at the corner of Manor Way; a nice easy walk and they came home to lunch. No school dinners until grammar school! Sports, such as they were, had to be played in the Pinn Fields. I remember my little girl winning a race held at the 1953 Coronation celebrations on the new running track at Kings College Road. She also danced round a maypole at the Manor Farm with Bishop Winnington-Ingram School.

Shopping was easy, all to hand just round the corner in the High Street, butchers, bakers, grocers, greengrocers, fishmonger, Woolworths, Lyttons and all. There was a small Sainsbury's near the corner of Ickenham Road, still with the beautiful tiles on the walls of country scenes with cows, and they served butter from a large lump into half or one pound blocks with fancy wooden patters.'

GETTING ABOUT

Travelling was a pleasure when the roads were quieter than they are today, and walking or bicycling was a regular feature of our lives. We look back with nostalgia, too, to those noisy but endearing trams.

42

A charabanc outing in 1912, a popular way of travelling on days out.

▨ TRAMS AND TROLLEY BUSES ▨

'We often had family outings from Southall to local places of interest, and we travelled everywhere by bus and trolley bus (along the Uxbridge Road). I used to love the trolley buses as they were so much quieter than the others. We were lucky, I suppose, living in an area covered by a relatively good and, mostly, frequent transport system – buses, trains and trolley buses, and the Underground of course, and we also had the river. I remember going to Richmond, where we often caught the boat. On this occasion we did not take a return trip but travelled to Westminster instead and back home by tube to Ealing and trolley bus to Southall. It seemed a sad day indeed when they took down all the posts and overhead wires from Uxbridge to Shepherds Bush and the "607" became just another bus route.'

'A tram ride was a treat, with the driver standing on the platform in front driving the tram by use of a big handle. Buses had no tops, if it rained it was hard luck, you either got off or put your coat over your head!'

'The trams with open tops had tarpaulins attached to the back of the seats so that when it rained they covered one's lower half. In the mid 1930s the fare from Palmers Green by trolley bus to the tube station and onward to South Kensington was 1s 6d return. My weekly wage then was about £1 10s.'

⬛ UXBRIDGE TRANSPORT ⬛

'My first glimpse of Uxbridge was the inside of the Great Western Railway station in Vine Street on a dark November night in 1939, and as I stepped out of the train I wondered where my parents had brought me to now. In later years my own children loved that railway, with its smokey old "push and pull" that they used to call "Daddy's train". The Underground station was, and still is, in the middle of the town, now the only station in Uxbridge.

Trolley buses ran between Uxbridge and Shepherds Bush. They had replaced the tramcars, but the lines were still on the High Street.

The roads after the war, as I recall, were fairly quiet as it was still unusual to own a car. I used to ride a bicycle to work, and for getting out and about at weekends. Now with motorways on three sides of Uxbridge, the M4, M25 and M40, it is a very different picture. Who had heard of traffic pollution then, or even pelican crossings? There have been many, many changes, but are they all for the better?'

'From being a busy place on the railway's map earlier in this century, Uxbridge has seen the decline of its importance until now it is left with a tube station only.

The main connection was to West Drayton from Vine Street and who will remember the Bowler and Umbrella Brigade who entrained at Cowley and detrained in the evening from a Paddington service?

By 1962 one daily coal train came from Southall to High Street,

Uxbridge, went on to Denham and back to Southall, its daily work finished at 1 pm.

Do you remember the railway bridge over the main road at Cowley? That's a long time ago, I hear you say – it is! Earlier still we had a station and another bridge in the High Street, with a grand plan to join up to West Drayton but, of course, that never occurred. Now I think all trace has gone. In fact the last passengers to use the High Street station were in an enthusiasts' special in September 1954.

The run up from West Drayton to Vine Street has lost its landmarks, but the small piece of cutting just below Cowley Bridge on the side of Brunel and Cleveland Roads still remains. It was originally intended to place a piece of wide gauge track in the cutting as a memorial to Brunel himself.'

▣ PROUD OWNER ▣

'Following a bad car accident I thought my doctor was mad when he suggested that the best way to cure my nervousness was to learn to drive. Me drive? I was never going to get in a car again! After much persuasion I started lessons, twelve guineas for twelve lessons, and was lucky enough to pass my test first time. At that time I was working for my boyfriend in the office of his building business, which had a large yard attached.

One day a strange car appeared in the yard. A customer of ours asked if we could store it until sold, as he had just bought a new car and did not have room for two. The fun then started. Every time one of the workmen came into the office they said, "Is that your car?" "She's not having a car," would be the response, while I nodded enthusiastically in the background. This went on for some time until, knowing he was beaten, he agreed that it would be mine.

I became the proud owner of an eleven year old car, one of the first available after the war, which had been driven by that old chestnut "one careful lady driver to go to church". It had genuinely only 9,000 miles on the clock. The only snag was the shock absorbers were not up to much and one was inclined to go up and down when travelling over slightly rough ground. How I loved that car! Even though I had not wanted to drive, the great feeling of being able to go anywhere without public transport or a lift was marvellous, although for quite a time I always had someone in the car with me.

Then came the day when I was alone in the office. The phone rang, it was one of the men in a panic – the customer was threatening to stop the job because of shortage of dust sheets. Knowing how important the customer was, without thinking, I loaded the car, locked the office, and off I went to deliver them. It was not until I was back in the office after a 20 mile round trip that it hit me. I had driven for the first time on my own. I could not stop shaking. After a calming cup of tea I thought I have done it once, I can do it again! The sense of achievement was immense. There was no stopping me then, I even drove the company van picking up and delivering materials when we were extra busy.

Since that time in 1960 I have driven various cars far, far better than that first "banger" but I do not think any of them have given me such pleasure as that old grey Austin A40.'

◼ BIKES AND CARS ◼

'In 1937 buses in Ruislip Manor were rather infrequent and pocket money was extremely limited so transport for me, a nine year old, meant roller skates. In those days most boys and even some girls possessed a pair. They could be bought as a complete unit from the Manor toy shop Bunces or as separate parts from Woolworths, with each part costing 6d.

Before the war most families seemed to own some sort of bicycle and in 1939 cycle shops were as commonplace as petrol stations are today. The cheapest model was an Elswick which cost £3 7s 6d whilst the top end of the range, the Raleigh and Rudge-Whitworth, were over £5. Any bike could be bought from the local cycle shop by paying a small deposit and the balance in weekly instalments which were recorded in the shopkeeper's book and also on a card kept by the purchaser. This system of hire purchase was colloquially known as the "never-never".

A bicycle became a necessity for me in the summer of 1939 as in the autumn I was to start my secondary education at a school which was halfway between Eastcote and Rayners Lane and there was no form of direct transport between house and school, which were some two miles apart. So it was that I became the proud owner of a secondhand but almost new BSA complete with semi-drop handlebars, saddlebag and lights. Also included in the price of £2 5s paid by my father was a full set of wet weather oilskins: leggings, cape and sou'-wester hat. There was no padlock and chain, such things were not necessary then!

Cars were a rarity in Ruislip Manor before the war and it was a time when schoolboys exhibited a prowess in controlling and riding their machines which would be impossible on our roads today. A whistling paperboy riding "no-handed" but in complete command of his bicycle was a frequent sight. Also not unusual was the "three boy bike" with one on the handlebars, one in a standing position and pedalling, with the third lad sitting on the saddle and urging the "engine room" to pedal faster!'

◈ Cows to Milk! ◈

'When we first came to live in Northwood Hills in 1944 the farm in Joel Street used to bring their cows over the main road to the fields behind our house. When it was time for milking they

would hold up the traffic to take them to the sheds and afterwards hold it up again to bring them back.'

❖ A PLEASURE TO WALK ❖

'I was born in Uxbridge in 1927 and perhaps my earliest memory is holding my father's hand as he swung me over water-filled ditches in Breakspeare Road on the way to visit my maternal grandmother who had the village shop in Ruislip some three miles away. Naturally, we also walked home.

Back in the early 1930s walking played a large part in our family's leisure activities; at that time children were not allowed to opt out of the weekend walk and our walks were not little constitutionals round the then beautifully kept Fassnidge Park. Five or six miles were considered to be a short walk and the sun didn't always shine; my mother insisted that my father could always find the muddiest footpaths. A very basic but sturdy perambulator enabled my parents to take us three girls aged two, four and six on many jaunts.

Exciting finds on our walks included the first sighting of the season for wild flowers – cowslips, ox-eye daisies, poppies, kingcups, harebells, violets, scabious, etc. Rabbits in the field ran like mad if Father clapped his hands.

During the period 1948 to 1954 I worked at West Drayton and initially a colleague and I walked to work but gradually the traffic built up and our efforts at keeping fit came to an end.

In the period 1955 to 1962 when my children were pre-school it was possible to walk along the river Frays – feed the ducks and watch grain being unloaded from barges at the mills at the bottom of the town – on up to Uxbridge Common by a small

farm to see the cows and then back down into the town to do the shopping before returning home.

Perambulators were now beautifully polished (black or navy), very sturdy and comfortable to push on long walks. The eldest child had a pedal scooter (purchased secondhand from an American service family) which could get up quite a speed and the traffic was still slight enough for safety.

Now Uxbridge is dissected by a relief road – the canal arm and mill covered by an office block; Fassnidge Park is unkept and vandalised; the farm is a housing estate. Most of the wild flowers have gone – the lovely buttercup meadow is now a golf course. It is no wonder that parents now have collapsible buggies to put in the car boot so that they are able to get out to more pleasant surroundings. Most of the footpaths and bridleways have survived but the whine of motorways is ever present.'

▨ THE PUSH AND PULL ▨

'At Northolt in 1939 there was no tube station. The train was called the "Push and Pull" and it went up to Ladbrook Road, London from the station and back, ninepence return. There was a small bridge over the lines to use when you got off the train, or if you had a pram they let you push it across the rails.'

THE GROWTH OF HEATHROW

▨ THE TWO RIVERS ▨

'Anyone who knows the area now is aware of the two man-made rivers that form the southern boundary of Heathrow airport. As a child growing up in the 1940s I remember the village of Heathrow that gave its name to this monstrosity and the former course of the Old River.

I lived in the hamlet of West Bedfont (one shop, one mission

In 1946 Heathrow airport welcomed passengers to canvas tents and caravans.

hall and one pub) in the parish of Stanwell. Later we became an extension of Long Lane. My early memories take me over the Duke of Northumberland (or First River as it was known) Bridge, that was wide enough to take motorised vehicles, although few were seen. Then northward, up High Tree Lane to the Old River (a good three-quarters of a mile) where there was just a footbridge and a watering hole crossing.

On one occasion we actually went to see an aeroplane that had crashed with its nose on the south bank and its tail on the north bank; it just managed to straddle the river. The passenger seats were still intact, numbering probably no more than ten.

Just a few years later I recall seeing the Brabazon fly overhead as it left Heathrow. This monster was capable of carrying passengers but was deemed too heavy for the purpose. A runway had to be reinforced just to receive it empty.

In the year of 1947 much fun was had on the frozen First River, only to be equalled by the ensuing hot summer. The banks of the river were declared to be as crowded as Brighton beach. That summer the watering hole became so shallow that with a skip you could clear the trickle of water in a couple of steps.

Time passed and Heathrow progressed until one memorable night when my mother was awakened from her sleep by the apparent headlights of a car heading for her first floor bedroom – that was the beginning of night flights.'

▣ WATCHING THE AIRPORT GROW ▣

'Occasionally my brother and I would play truant from Sunday school and walk along the Bath Road from Cranford to see how the airport was progressing. The nearness of aircraft to the pavements would not be tolerated now, for security as well as noise restrictions. The airline logos on the sides of these machines fascinated us. By writing to the companies direct at the airport we applied for and received the most magical packets of timetables, postcards, and best of all, large posters of the planes, with cut-away details of the seating plans and engines. Two of these posters decorated my bedroom wall for two years, I remember how proud I was of my Douglas DC4 decor.

As flights increased, so did the traffic. In 1960 the Bath Road through Harmondsworth, Harlington and Cranford was widened up to the junction with the Great West Road at Hounslow West. Several roadside buildings had to go, including my father's local pub, the Stag and Hounds. My diary records how upset he was. He was even more upset when the first of the hotels went up, the Ariel at Harlington Corner, taking over the place where the Coach and Horses stood.

The airport began to take over, more hotels went up and again my father's anger was recorded in my diary when the old Bricklayer's Arms at Harmondsworth was renamed the "Air Hostess" in May 1954. As a child I had often walked along the Bath Road to the Bricklayer's. My Dad told me it had belonged to a famous cricketer, but I remember it for the old pear tree in the garden, and being given a sackful of pears to take home. The cricketer, I found out years later, was Jack Hearne who played for Middlesex and England. The Air Hostess was later demolished to make way for offices.

All the air passengers making their way from the airport to London travelled along the Bath Road. It seemed that there was always someone in the know as to who was arriving, who was of any consequence. A "bush telegraph" buzzed that a film star was on his or her way, or even more exciting, Royalty. Crowds would turn up along the road in Cranford to wave at large black cars containing celebrities.

On 8th March 1955, in falling snow, I pushed a pram containing my 13 month old son to the top of Waye Avenue, Cranford to wave to Princess Margaret as she went by. I don't know where she had been but she was wearing a yellow outfit and she had a tan. The cars always slowed down for the wavers. Then I trudged back home and two hours later I produced a daughter. My husband registered her as Margaret because he didn't like the names I had chosen, and Margaret came readily to mind.

More and more air traffic crowded the Bath Road. It wasn't until 1962 that work started on the M4 motorway, and again Middlesex had to bear the brunt of traffic progress. The upheavals of the building of Heathrow had to lead on to major road building. Cranford Park was halved in area. Where once the pretty church of St Dunstan stood in the centre of parkland, it now stands beside the motorway.

The celebrities went to London from the airport along the new route. In any case, television appearances of the famous made us all quite blasé about who was who, and even without the M4 I don't think anyone would have bothered to congregate to wave. Most local people worked or had work connected with the airport by the 1970s.

A great deal of Middlesex farmland and smallholdings have been obliterated by Heathrow airport, many old buildings and homes had to go, but it has provided work and a lot of revenue, not just for Middlesex but for the country too. Whether we like it or nor we have to accept the airport and the motorway; after all, neither I nor my family have moved away from it.'

'On a Sunday afternoon I would cycle over and park up alongside the wire fence on the Bath Road and watch the planes arriving, hoping to see famous people going to and fro between the planes and the wooden arrival and departure huts which were situated close to that edge of the airport. This was before it became so large. Some of the white wooden huts are still there just beyond the new telephone exchange building.'

❖ COMET AND CONCORDE ❖

'I was married in March 1952 and first lived in a bedsitter in Strawberry Hill. I remember well the day in May when the first Comet jet was due to take off on its first commercial flight from Heathrow. I had the radio on, and was ready to run to the window after it took off. But the amazing thing was that the Comet passed overhead (a different sound to any heard before) before the commentary started. This was so that if there was a disaster on take off it would not be heard on the radio! Twenty four years later, 1976, living in Ashford, I remember waiting for the Concorde to take off from Heathrow on its first commercial flight, and can recall the thrill of seeing this swan-like machine rise into the sky.'

❖ WORKING AT THE AIRPORT ❖

'In March 1956 I went for an interview with the personnel department of the British Overseas Airways Corporation at London Airport. This was housed in a two floored building close to the end of No 1 runway. I was offered a job in the stores department which was situated in No 1 Hangar. This was one of the original hangars that had been used when the airport was first built and it stood in the middle of the airfield.

When I was at my desk typing I could see the empty aircraft taxi by the window on their way to pick up passengers to fly them all over the world. My job at that time was to type the declaration forms which accompanied the stores that were sent abroad to other company offices, etc.

Every eighth working day each typist was expected to work until 8 pm. This was compulsory overtime. It was rather scary cycling home in the dark, along a narrow path with fields either side of you and no street lights, only a bicycle lamp to show the way, until you reached the roadway that ran through the airport from the Bath Road to the Great West Road, now called Hatton's Corner. I always dreaded that an aircraft would come along the runway nearby but luckily it never did. This hangar can still be seen from the roadway. I only lasted there for two months. I used to bribe my boyfriend to come and meet me on his bike on these evenings!'

'Heathrow had been originally a test field for Fairey Aviation, then used during the Second World War as a military airfield. When I came to Heathrow, it was fast developing into an international airport, swallowing up three lovely little villages in the process. However, one could then still get to parts now closed to the public, and I well remember one rather misty Sunday afternoon cycling along what I thought was a new wide road, only to find it was an extension to the main runway! The passenger terminals were pretty primitive at that time, being marquees and tents; the administration offices were converted Nissen huts, and the aircraft maintenance areas were old RAF hangars.

Aircraft have developed so rapidly in our lifetime too, and we have seen the progress from little "prop jobs" to jets, and on to supersonic transport; from two seaters to jumbo jets. I recall when the first Pan Am jumbo flew into Heathrow. All the offices and buildings overlooking the main runway were crammed with people looking out – it was a wonder the buildings did not tip over. As the giant aircraft roared into the airport and touched down, we all gasped in amazement at the sheer size of it. Subsequently, of course, a "stretch" version developed, and jumbos are normal to us, so we look with interest now at the little executive jets that whizz in and out.'

'I came to Middlesex, newly married in 1963. Alan and I bought a house on the A4 Bath Road, Harlington and we have lived there ever since. It was the main roadway to Heathrow airport for passengers so all London traffic came by the house. It was a busy road and word got around if a VIP was due or leaving the airport. People would line the street outside and we would watch the big black cars glide by from our bedroom window, only finding out afterwards from the papers who we had been waving to. To me, a country girl, it was all very exciting. This was the Beatles and later the Bay City Rollers era and fans of these groups (mainly girls) would stream up to the airport on foot to catch a glimpse of their heroes. The girls dressed in their tartan trousers and scarves (fans of the Bay City Rollers) are particularly memorable.

At this time the M4 was being constructed. When it was finally opened all our traffic disappeared and the road was very peaceful apart from the occasional car which must have been local traffic. Not many of us had cars then so the streets kept reasonably safe for my children. Now, alas, the M4 and the A4 are chock-a-block and accidents outside on the busy Bath Road are quite commonplace.'

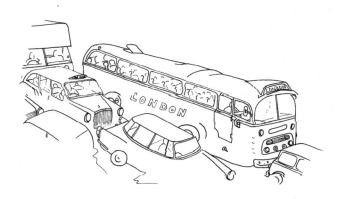

HOUSE & HOME

THE WAY WE LIVED THEN

Memories of Middlesex life from the turn of the century, and during the building of the new estates that transformed so much of the old rural county – setting up home and meeting new neighbours from all parts of the country. Housework was hard and labour intensive, with few mod cons to lighten the load.

◉ LIFE IN THE ALMSHOUSES ◉

'The Reverend Rowland Hill was the minister at Surrey Chapel in Blackfriars (this place of worship later moved to the present site to become Christ Church), and in 1811 Rowland Hill was responsible for the building of the first almshouses at Blackfriars in London for the poor spinsters and widows of Lambeth and Southwark.

In 1894 they were preparing to move from their site at Blackfriars and new almshouses were built on land in Feltham Hill Road, Ashford, Middlesex. This land was given by one Nellie Earl Attlee, the foundation stone of the Rowland Hill Almshouses was laid on 12th July 1894 and the move was accomplished in 1895.

The new almshouses were built on opposite sides of a square and joined at the back of the square by a red brick building which contained a common room and kitchen and over the top a flat for visitors. This flat had a bathroom and I remember the bath, WC and washbasin were patterned with flowers.

The almshouses were built as tall terraced double-fronted houses and each house contained four flats (two on the ground floor and two upstairs), and one shared toilet. The flats contained a medium sized living room, single bedroom and a very small kitchen. In 1895 the flats were sparsely furnished and in the bedrooms there was a single iron bedstead and a combined washstand with attached chest of drawers. For hanging clothes

The Rowland Hill Almshouses at Ashford.

there were three coat hooks in the corner of the bedroom – being poor you were not expected to have many clothes. In each living room there was a cooking range for heating and cooking and the residents were given two hundredweight of coal each week for this purpose. In addition they lived rent and rates free and were given six shillings per week to live on in addition to the coal supplied.

To qualify for an almshouse you had to be a poor spinster or widow and belong to a nonconformist or free church. The original ladies also had to wear black clothing with a shawl round their shoulders and crossing over their front and their long black skirts had to come to the top of their boots (no trace of leg to be shown). Another rule was that they were not allowed to be away from their flat for more than ten days in any year.'

A Southall terraced house, with its iron railings still intact before they were taken for the war effort.

◆ Born in Jubilee Year ◆

'My earliest memory is of my mother telling me that I was a "Victorian baby" as I was born in the year of Queen Victoria's Diamond Jubilee. In due course I was told of the Queen's spectacular funeral and Edward VII's accession and coronation which was postponed owing to his illness; I half remember that it was appendicitis, which became fashionable, so it was said.

My father was manager of a large nursery some two miles

from the historic town of Enfield. He lived on the job so our home was a very old house – nearly 200 years. The front was covered with the two varieties of jasmine, the sweetly scented white in the summer, and the yellow variety gave a welcome splash of colour in the winter. A grapevine grew on the sunny side; the grapes were different from the hot-house kind, but my mother made a delicious preserve with them.

Of course the house had some disadvantages, but its great advantage was its warmth and cosiness and special atmosphere. The walls were quite thick. There were latches to some of the doors, others had brass knobs which had to be polished. There were two staircases – the top room was large and airy, nice to sleep in when occasion demanded. The most fascinating room was the kitchen/dining room, as the only kitchen feature was the large open range with its open fire, trivets and hobs on which a kettle seemed always to be singing, and an oven, no, two ovens in which my mother cooked our delicious, wholesome meals. But the Christmas turkey was not cooked in the oven, but on a spit or jack in front of the fire and we children took turns in turning it round so that it was evenly cooked. To keep the range looking really nice it had to be polished with black lead, the hearth cleaned with white hearthstone and the fire-irons, which were made of steel, polished until they looked like silver. The sitting room had a wide arched open grate, very pretty with brass fire-irons and coal bucket (more polishing!). The coal, of good quality Derby Brights, was brought by the coalman in sacks every week and emptied into the coal cellar ready for use. Green Venetian blinds had to be carefully washed and the Nottingham white lace curtains looked lovely – they needed careful laundering.

In the sitting room were two easy chairs, one for Father and one for Mother. Significantly, Father's chair had arms so that he could relax and go to sleep or read the paper. Mother's chair had no arms, so she didn't find it easy to relax, but perhaps she wasn't expected to, because she always had a pile of mending to do and many pairs of woollen socks to darn, so the arms would prevent her own arms' freedom of movement.

A very important room was the kitchen/scullery which

contained the stone sink, with one cold water tap (no hot water, of course, but we were lucky in having water laid on), although we did have an outside "loo" with water. The scullery also contained pots and pans, food safes, two large tables, and the large white copper which was lit every Monday morning in order to heat the water in which white clothes and table linen were boiled.

You will have gathered that when we were young we had no gas or electricity, although years later gas was laid on and a gas cooker was added to our kitchen equipment. My mother never really took to it for baking, and the cakes, especially rich fruit cakes, baked in the open range were lovely and very popular with our friends who came to Sunday tea. Oil lamps and candles were our means of lighting and how beautiful most of them were, candlesticks of painted porcelain, or filigreed brass. We children carried a lighted candle upstairs to bed, with never an accident – we were so carefully trained. The lamps made a lot of work, filling them with oil which had to be kept in a safe place, cleaning the glass chimneys, which sometimes got blackened with soot, trimming or changing the wick and polishing the brass lamps themselves. They gave an adequate light so there was no problem with reading or writing.

This reminds me that when as a family we had been out together and came home in the dark, my father used to say, as we stood at the back door, "Now stay where you are while I go in and light the lamp." It was not until we saw the soft glow of lamplight that we were allowed inside.

We were fortunate, as children, in spending a month at my Granny's in a village in Kent. It was long enough for us to become part of the village life, playing games with the children, sampling a day in the hop fields, being invited to the Harvest Homes in the "gentry's" lovely estates, going to church and Sunday school, etc. But what surprised us was to see the girls bobbing a curtsey to those same "gentry" whenever they met them or saw them riding in their lovely carriages – the boys gave a stiff bow from the waist and doffed their caps. We did *not* follow suit.

For boys and girls their mid-teens birthday was very important for it was the day when girls put their hair up. This was a great change from the fashion of tying it back with wide black silk ribbon. They also wore ankle length skirts and dresses. Boys went into trousers – "long-uns" as they were called. These were signs that childhood was left behind, they were now growing up.

A year or two before the First World War, when walking behind two ladies: "Oh! just look at those ladies, they seem to be only shuffling along." Yes, they *were* hobbling along, wearing the ridiculous hobble skirts. The war put an end to those as women took over men's jobs. Can you imagine trying to get up the stairs of a double-decker bus if you were a conductress?

During the early period of the 20th century, in spite of some national hardships, families like mine lived happy lives with no thought that they could be interrupted in any way, but alas on the 4th August 1914 war was declared with Germany and everything changed, a new era began.

Looking back over that world which was different from today, so different that it has to be almost unbelievable, I find that I was in a world which in spite of the lack of amenities which we consider necessary and take for granted today, had much to recommend it. Life was simpler, more stable, less complicated than the present.'

▣ STATION HOUSE, STRAWBERRY HILL ▣

'My earliest recollections go back to the year 1927 when I went to live with my grandparents at the Station House, Strawberry Hill. This was a large rambling place without a bathroom – the bath was under the hinged scullery table and had to be filled with hot water from the copper boiler. The only lavatory was in the lobby outside the back door and for one's convenience during the night one reached under the bed!

The weekly washing was done in the copper, then rinsed in the sink and finally put through the mangle. This was one of my jobs during the school holidays and from an early age I had regular tasks to do for which I received twopence a week. Although we had gas lighting downstairs, we used candles to light our way upstairs. The house was heated by open coal fires downstairs and most of the cooking was done on the kitchen range.

Apart from the large Victorian houses in the neighbouring roads, Strawberry Hill was just a village with four small shops and the railway station. In fact most of the areas bordering Twickenham were rural. I remember the superb house and estate belonging to King Manuel of Portugal and the large estates of Riversdale House, Radnor House and Poulett Lodge in Cross Deep.

Hanworth, where I live now, was deep in countryside and inaccessible by public transport. In fact, when the Graf Zeppelin landed in the Air Park in 1924 we walked from Strawberry Hill to see it.

Eel Pie Island, Twickenham was another landmark and before the Second World War we often went across the ferry to dances at the "Casino". Very draughty in mid-winter when dressed in a long flimsy outfit.

Going back to household affairs, I recall that food was really good, though I must admit that the regular weekly menu never varied. It was roast beef on Sunday; cold beef and bubble and squeak on Monday; cottage pie on Tuesday; lamb stew on Wednesday; liver and bacon on Thursday; fish on Friday and sausages and mash on Saturday. Cullens the grocer came every Monday for the weekly order and the local butcher, baker and greengrocer delivered daily.

Housework was also tackled on a regular basis, each day of the week being set aside for specific jobs. Sunday, however, was a day of rest and as a child I found it the longest time of the week. The one redeeming feature was that very often relatives came to tea on Sunday afternoon.

Clothes and fashion were no problem for me as a growing child because I had to wear what was bought for me and quite honestly I did not mind. However, from the time I became a teenager, or a "young lady" as we were termed then, I rose to the height of fashion by being allowed to wear beige rayon stockings instead of black woollen ones! Permanent waving became more widely available and in 1937 I endured three hours of discomfort having my hair wound in metal curlers and being strung up to some contraption in order to emerge looking like a golliwog!

I must conclude by saying life seemed less stressful in those times and we hardly ever had to visit the doctor. Though I must add that his charge was five shillings a visit, so we were nearly at death's door before going to the surgery.'

◈ PATTERNS ON THE WINDOW ◈

'The patterns on the window, inside and out, made strange shapes of leaves and flowers, intricate facets beautifully formed. It was cosy in bed and warm and it took a time to jump out, grab a dressing gown and clothes, find slippers on the bedside mat and hurry downstairs to the warmth of the kitchen and the fire range. Mum was cooking our breakfast and Dad was on the way out to work, cycling over the crunching snow to the railway station to catch the 8.01 am train to London.

My brother and I would venture outside later to play in the snow. "Build a snowman – run around," encouraged our Mum, "you'll soon be warm." But we weren't! Twenty minutes or so later we came indoors, hands and feet icy cold and painfully thawing out. The coal fire was welcoming.

The coal in our house in the 1920s was housed in the "indoor" coal cellar next to the loo. In cold weather a lighted night light was placed on a saucer in the loo at night and covered with a terracotta flower pot. This stopped the pipes from freezing and it was surprising how warm the "little house" felt next morning. The pantry cum larder was *very* cold – no need for freezers or fridges in winter then. The milk often had a thin film of ice on the surface. Milk was kept in jugs and covered with netting edged with beads.

Winter weather called for hot filling meals – home-made soup, neck of lamb and rabbit stews, roly poly and treacle puddings and thick slices of toast for tea with butter. It was much better toasting in front of an open fire using a long-handled brass toasting fork and you could choose from lightly, medium or well toasted slices. Each slice was carefully stacked on a plate by the hearth and kept warm. On Monday and Tuesday there was a pot of dripping to spread on slices – dig down for the jelly in pork dripping. Crumpets were good oozing with butter and lightly sprinkled with salt. Bread and milk for supper with brown sugar and sultanas – a good remedy for colds too.

Friday night was bath night. In winter the large tin bath was on a thick towel in front of the kitchen range fire. All very cosy but one couldn't touch the side nearest to the fire after a while, it became too hot.

In summer time water had to be pumped up to the bathroom to fill the copper geyser at the end of the bath. It took 72 "pumps" from the sink to fill that geyser and the main water was diverted by turning off the cold water tap in the kitchen sink. The bathroom ceiling sloped towards the window so one had to stoop down or kneel to look out of it. There was so much room that in autumn the apples were stored there – you checked the apples and turned them over while you dried yourself after a bath.'

▓ THE GREAT WOOD SCRAMBLE OF 1928 ▓

'If you stand at the corner of Laleham Road and Watersplash Road at Shepperton Green and look down Watersplash Road you will see houses on either side of the road with hardly room for one more building. A few years ago a company wishing to excavate gravel from a field at the back of the houses on the right-hand side of the road offered all householders free double glazing to help them keep out the expected noise from the workings. In 1928 it would have cost them very little. From the top of the road where you are standing to the river Ash at the bottom there were hardly more than ten buildings including a public house (the Hope) and a church (St John's).

Walking down Watersplash Road and looking between the buildings the trees of a vast orchard could be seen. This great orchard was known to us as Leonard's Fields. The area it covered

ran from Laleham Road on one side, the whole length of Watersplash Road, then following the path of the river Ash (known to all as "The Splash") to Charlton Road. Around 1928 the whole area was taken over by a market garden company called Barker's. Almost overnight it became Barker's Fields. It was decided that the trees would have to come down and this led to "The Great Watersplash Road Wood Scramble".

The most modern equipment was called in to carry out the operation and soon many trees were uprooted, so many in fact that the work must have been held up with too many trees already felled getting in the way. The problem was solved by inviting anyone wanting wood to "come and get it". Everyone used wood for fires and although the coalman delivered coal each week at 2s 6d per hundredweight, extra free wood was a cheap alternative.

Soon the area was crowded with industrious people working with saws and axes of all descriptions. Chunks of tree were taken away to be cut up at home whilst most people had a barrow of some sort which was filled with logs and trundled to a shed in the back garden. The trees taken away could hardly keep up with the trees being pulled down. Everyone seemed to want plum wood which experts said burned better. It was a real family affair, everyone helping out, although not necessarily each other.

Mr Barker must have been happy with the situation. I suppose he was a bit of a philanthropist in a way, I am sure that if the same thing happened today a contractor would be involved and the public kept out.

It was summer and the weather was hot and dry. Most work by the local people went on in the evenings after tea or dinner and during the weekend; Father filled the barrows and the boys took the barrows home to unload. After about three weeks only piles of sawdust remained. All the roots from the apples and plum trees had been burned leaving nothing behind except the charred earth. Our shed was filled to capacity with enough logs to light and sustain our fires for months to come.

I was just seven at the time and spent many hours in the field helping my father. I remember holding the other end of a cross-cut to keep it steady as my father worked away. As for the year. Anyone who could whistle was trying to capture the melody of the first talking picture, *The Jazz Singer* with Al Jolson singing "...when there are grey skies – I don't mind the grey skies..." *Sonny Boy* was all the rage. It was a beautiful summer.'

▣ SOME THINGS DON'T CHANGE ▣

'Twice recently drivers of plain vans have called over to me, "Do you live around here?" Thinking they wanted directions I have responded – but they have tried to whisper, "I have been laying a carpet and have a piece over, which you can have cheap."

As soon as we moved in to Sudbury in 1934, two men arrived with a roll of lino. They had been "laying lino in the show house", which did not exist, "and could sell this roll". They pushed their way in, unrolling the lino and cutting off Mother and me as they made their way along the wall to the backroom door. As they went to open the door, I was surprised to hear my mother say, "You open that door and you will have a bull terrier at your throat." (Her purse was on the bureau just inside.) As the door knob was touched Jimmy, a usually friendly cross brindle terrier, growled and began to bark. The lino was quickly rolled up, but left for "husband" to see. A workman came downstairs and told Mother that they were up to no good. When they returned, he was scraping paint off floorboards behind the front door. Mother told them to be off with their lino and one glanced behind the door and said, "Oh it was you who put her up to it, was it?"

We were also sold "tulip" trees and other exotic plants which eventually had to be uprooted.'

🔹 No Fridge 🔹

'When I was a little girl we had no fridge, washing machine or hot running water. Mother kept milk and dairy produce in a large meat safe. This had a wooden back and three sides of wire mesh. The holes were minute to keep flies out yet allow air to circulate. The safe stood on the floor. Jellies were left to set by standing the moulds in cold water. Milk was also kept this way in the summer. There was no year-round ice cream. One of my Saturday treats was being given a lump of ice to suck by our fishmonger.

🔹 The First Estates 🔹

'During the 1930s many of the green fields of Middlesex disappeared to be replaced by huge housing estates. They seemed to spring up everywhere and almost overnight it seemed. Thousands of ordinary working folk left London and elsewhere to live on these estates, at last able to buy a house of their own for as little as £375. Our small family, father, mother and myself, moved to Ruislip Manor early in 1937 and into a brand new house in a terrace of six built by the George Ball Estate Company.

Although basically only two up and two down (two bedrooms and two living rooms), it boasted the luxury of a separate bathroom as well as a small kitchen with in-built cupboards and, in estate agent parlance, a kitchenette. It measured approximately nine feet by six feet and according to Mother was not big enough to swing a kitten in, let alone a cat. Despite this drawback, which mystified me as we didn't possess either, the house was a veritable heaven compared to the flat that had been our home in Fulham. We now lived in the "country". We had two gardens, one at the front as well as one at the back and neighbours were only either side of us and not above and below as well, all for £425: a deposit of £25 and the balance on a 21 year mortgage.

Each room had a fireplace, including the two bedrooms, and hot water was via a "boot" or back boiler fitted behind the rear downstairs room fireplace with coal as the fuel. In winter the fire would be damped down overnight with wet tea leaves (no tea bags in those days) so that in the morning the still live embers could be used to rekindle the fire. The houses costing £375 had no kitchenette and the rear room formed what today would be termed a kitchen/diner, their hot water provided by a small Ideal free-standing boiler mounted on a tile base in the corner of the room.'

▣ STILL BEING BUILT ▣

'When I first came to Enfield I was 13 years old. Our house was one of a new estate, the farmland on which it was built having belonged to Cambridge University. There were some of the houses with parts of their back gardens still unfenced because a public path ran through them and until the path was diverted the fencing could not go up.

There was a wooden arch across the bottom of the road to attract would-be buyers and houses were still being built. There was a path at the back of our garden with a high hedge, but there were several holes where we kids could crawl through. Once through we explored the grounds of this lovely house soon to be pulled down. There was a lake with a rough iron bridge over, a big fruit garden and many a fruit pie was made by our mums.

Opposite our road there was Flemings Farm with the field at the front, now a swimming pool, but the farm building is still there and used by the park attendants. When we all first arrived, Mr Flemings left everyone a free pint of milk each day for a week and a pot of cream on Sunday, hoping he would get our custom.

At the bottom of the road, along the main road was a blacksmith's and either side of the smithy were little wooden cottages, but alas all gone. Further along was the Bell where it is said Dick Turpin stopped on his way to Ware. Opposite was the little Co-op shop with several cottages alongside and the local cinema on the corner.'

◈ NEW NEIGHBOURS ◈

'In May 1936 the third section of Birchway, Hayes was nearly completed and the new tenants were allowed to move in. I remember the day well. There were about six removal vans in the road all unloading furniture, and both adults and children were interested to see who their new neighbours would be. Most of them came from areas of London, we came from South Wales. The only thing everyone had in common was that the man of the house worked for the Great Western Railway. This section of road was finally finished in 1937.

We had only been in the house for about a week when a group of real gypsies came around selling pegs. Recognising that my mother's accent was different from the others they asked her if she would let them have some water, which my mother did. You can imagine our surprise, looking out of the front window later, to see the gypsies sitting on the pavement outside our house, around a fire that they had lit from paper and wood collected from the nearby building site, brewing a pot of tea and eating their food. This did not do much good for my mother's image, who had already been dubbed the "Welsh woman" at number 98, although actually my mother and father were both Devonians.

Things soon settled down and when the neighbours all got to know each other they became great friends and helped each other when they had problems. It was a lovely life for the children too, because there were so many of us around the same age. It did not matter whether you had brothers or sisters because we went everywhere together as a group, to school, to the park, picnics, and later the cinema and dances. It was only when we started courting, and eventually got married, that some of us lost touch with each other.

After the war ended each section of the street had a large party to celebrate this and also the safe return of the husbands and sons who were in the forces. We were lucky, so far as I can remember every one of them came home unhurt. The wives all planned together to provide the food, although rationing was still in being, soft drinks were provided and something a little stronger for the adults. There were games for children and adults alike, the old tug-of-war was very funny. A piano was brought out from one of the houses for a sing-along, and later an old wind-up gramophone and records were produced for dancing. As the evening progressed all the parties got together into one.

About this time there was a large bonfire in the field at the top end of Birchway, where the Fina petrol station now stands opposite Caswell & Pickups chemist. To celebrate the end of the war one of the chemists, I believe it was Mr Pickup, produced his home-made fireworks. He would not let anyone else set them off, but what fun, some of the younger children had never seen fireworks before.'

◙ SETTING UP HOME ◙

'I was married on 4th December 1948. From London we caught a train to Shepperton and walked along Green Lane to a bungalow for which my parents had lent us the money – £2,600! I found a little book the other day in which I had written details of my trousseau, which had cost £68 15s 11d. This included £7 for my wedding dress, £9 9s for my "costume", and £2 12s 6d for "parachute for undies".

I had also kept a record of virtually every item of furniture we bought, the total cost of £296 15s. A dining table and four chairs cost £14 10s 9d; a wardrobe £26 18s; a carpet £30; a radio £20 8s 10d; and a bed (Utility) £7 10s.

In 1953 we bought our first car. It was a secondhand Ford Eight (black) and cost £200.'

'In the mid 1950s we were still busy getting a decent home together after the shortages of the war years. Wonderful new kitchen appliances were beginning to go on sale in the shops and I well remember the excitement of buying our first refrigerator and the joy of being able to keep ice cream for use as and when required, followed by that wonder of wonders, the twin-tub washing machine. Tupperware made its appearance and nearly every "young married" held a Tupperware party to tempt us to buy smart containers for our store cupboard – a great step forward from jam jars!'

▣ An End of Terrace in Alperton ▣

'Married in 1953, we moved into an end-of-terrace three bedroomed house in Alperton, adjacent to the Grand Union Canal. Our house price was £2,250 and we struggled to raise the necessary 10% deposit. My husband's salary as a plumbing and heating surveyor was then £12 per week and we had no car. He travelled to work on the Piccadilly line to Hammersmith daily.

The rateable value of residences was determined by the location and local circumstances and we had one of the lowest rates as we had factories and a very tall chimney opposite – this was demolished in the mid 1960s.

One day during the 1960s on answering a ring at the front door one morning, I was confronted by a "Snowman" in full white fur outfit who asked me "if I knew the slogan". Luckily I did know and answered him correctly upon which he presented me with a crisp £5 note. To explain – Proctor & Gamble were running a sales promotion for Fairy Snow washing powder and everyone who was visited, who could tell the Snowman the slogan and show a packet of Fairy Snow, was rewarded with a cash prize.

Things were hard just then with three young children and I needed so many personal items that I remember keeping that £5 note for many months before deciding what to spend it upon!

I had my first washing machine – a Hoover twin tub model – in about 1966, having managed since marrying with the kitchen sink, a glass washboard and a secondhand spin dryer.'

◙ OUR TURKEY ◙

'In the 1950s my mother retired from her greengrocer's shop in Yiewsley, and we kept rabbits, chickens and pigs for our own consumption. One year after a visit to the market, my mother brought home six fertilised turkey eggs and put them under a broody hen. We had four turkeys hatch and they were fed on scraps and kept in the backyard. When Christmas time came three turkeys were killed and one was on our table, the other two distributed to other members of the family. One turkey remained destined for the Easter table.

This turkey grew and grew and was very vicious. It used to peck us in the back of the knee every time we went into the yard to feed the animals or garden. Everyone was afraid of it. It chased the postman away from the house and no one would enter the garden. By the time Easter came the turkey was huge. My mother could not get near it to wring its neck nor my father (who was a butcher), so they used my brother's air rifle to stun the poor thing. Then he was prepared for the oven. However, he was too big to go in the oven, so was taken to my uncle's baker's shop in Cranford and baked in the bread oven there. On Easter Sunday when all the family were gathered round the table we all talked about what this turkey had done to us, but there were so many memories no one could eat the meat. I expect an awful lot of him was put into the pig bin for the swill man to collect.'

WASHDAY

Few words can evoke such memories of sheer hard work as 'washday' – usually a Monday and a full day of steam, washing, rinsing, starching, blueing, mangling, drying and ironing. Water was a precious commodity, to be fetched from the well or pump.

◩ 'TWAS ON A MONDAY MORNING ◩

'Few married women worked. Housework was a full-time task. Dust from coal fires caused daily dusting and polishing. Rugs had to be shaken out of doors. In the spring carpets were taken up, laid over the line and beaten with a special cane beater. In between, a Ewbank carpet sweeper was used, while a stiff brush and pan were used on the stair carpet with each stair rod being removed and replaced in turn. There was also a weekly ritual of cleaning stone steps at the front door – my father arranged for a wooden one, covered by a metal plate, but even this needed meticulous polishing along with the letter box and house number. Indoor brass ornaments and a fender were cleaned weekly with Brasso and the silver-plated spoons and forks were shone with Silvo, while the steel blades of knives were sharpened on a stone until they wore down to stiletto points.

We used to sing a song: "Twas on a Monday morning, when I beheld my darling…" Washday – usually Mondays – involved boiling, in an open topped gas copper, rinsing, starching and whitening with Reckitt's "Dolly" blue in the final rinse. Then came mangling, hanging out to dry, folding, ironing, airing… and by then it was almost Sunday again, when, after the weekly Saturday hot bath, came newly washed clothes and the

---

Water had to be carried to the house every day – the water pump at Ickenham in 1913.

memorable delight of snuggling between freshly washed linen or cotton sheets. Blankets were washed in the bath on a sunny summer day with sufficient breeze to dry them out of doors.

There were several tradesmen who called, including the laundry but there were charges for each item and only a weekly collection. Father's stiff collars were sent away, until those with stiffeners were purchased. These were home washed, the greasy part first needing a scrub, then rinsed, ironed flat, carefully folded, ironed at either end along the fold, and finally at the centre – the stiffeners were then replaced.

Handkerchieves were first well soaked in salty water and then boiled. Ironing of these took time, as they often had to be redamped. I recall being taught to lay them flat, right side downwards, design in top right-hand corner, and iron over. Then bring the bottom to the top, but not quite, and iron over again. Some needed a further fold.'

▣ PAYING EXTRA ▣
'Up until the early 1960s there was a laundry named Brown's Laundry in Windmill Road, Sunbury on Thames, which dried its washing out of doors. On fine days as you went by you could see rows of billowing washing. I think you paid extra for having it dried outside.'

▣ THE WATER PUMP ▣
'My grandparents lived in a small house in the country, where the outside water pump supplied water for all domestic purposes: cooking, watering the somewhat large garden, usually full of vegetables and old-fashioned flowers, washing clothes and, of course, bathing in the tin bath tub, which would be placed by the open fire on winter's evenings. The water would be brought indoors in a large tin bucket, the contents heated, then poured into the bath tub, albeit only half full.

The water was always cool, sweet and refreshing to the palate on a hot summer's day, or any day really. Now water is pumped into the house, through the usual water system and the pump is no longer in operation as it was 70 years ago.'

▣ SHEER HARD WORK ▣
'Washing day was sheer hard work. Early morning Mother would light the fire under the copper with odd pieces of wood, mostly tar blocks, which was what the roads were made of. If repairs were being done, we would stand and wait to see if any of these blocks were split, then we were allowed to have them. I am ashamed to admit this, but when Mother was desperate for

wood, we would creep out at night and steal some. The clothes were put in to boil and poked down with a copper stick, some Hudson's washing powder was added. The clothes were then rinsed and a bowl of "blue" water was made, using a small muslin bag filled with blue powder. If net curtains were washed they were also dipped but in a cream coloured water (these were called "dolly dips").

Our large mangle seemed to weigh tons. One of us put the washing through and one turned the handle. The water gushed down into a tin bath, which had to be lugged out into the garden to empty it. White pieces of starch had boiling water put on them and when melted, collars and pillowcases were dipped into it. Clothes were then damped down after drying and rolled, not folded, for a couple of hours before being ironed. The iron was heated on the gas stove, or on a small shelf which was on the fire front. I used to watch and wait for my mother to spit on the iron to see if it was hot enough, standing well back in case it flew over on to me!

Saturday was the day for newspapers to be cut into squares and threaded on to a piece of string and hung in the lavatory. Only posh people had real toilet paper.'

▣ HOW I HATED IT! ▣

'How I hated washday! It was always on Mondays, but really started on Sunday evenings when my mother would gather up the wash to be done and the fire under the stone copper was laid ready to be lit at 5.30 the next morning. The copper dominated the scullery, together with the mangle, which to a small child looked like an instrument of torture.

Sunday was the "big feed" day when most households had a roast dinner, and teatime was also a big spread when my brother would bring his current girlfriend to tea. There was always plenty of food over because, of course, Monday was the dreaded day when I would come home from school at mid-day to find the house bathed in steam. If it was a fine day some of the washing would be outside on the line, but if it was raining it was hanging everywhere. I would pull a face at the inevitable cold meat and pickles and cold rice pudding, but did feel a pang when I saw Mother up to her elbows at the rubbing board. I was reminded however that I was lucky to have a dinner at all as some of the children in the street were less fortunate.

I clearly remember the day my father knocked the stone copper down and a new grey enamel gas boiler was installed. The mangle went also and a modern rubber-roller wringer took its place, but washday still went on. At least, however, Mother did not have to get up at 5.30 am on Monday and the copper did not have to be hearth-stoned after the "slavery" of washday.

I often think of those days when I flick the switch of the automatic washing machine, and, if it is raining, what the heck, there is the tumble-dryer.'

▨ How Convenient ▨

'Monday was always washday in the 1930s, no matter what the weather was like. When we came home from school the whole house smelled like a laundry. The washing was first boiled in a gas-fired copper, then rinsed in the sink, put through the hand-turned mangle and hung out in the garden to dry if the weather was fine. In bad weather, the washing was dried in front of the open fire in the living room or on the pulley airer above the gas cooker. Finally it was ironed with flat irons and left on the clothes horse to air for several days.

My mother purchased her first electric washing machine about 1950, a large cumbersome piece of equipment manufactured by Servis. Electricity had been installed in our part of Willesden (now the London Borough of Brent) in about 1935. By the year I was married, 1957, washing machines had become much slimmer and I bought a Hoover model followed by a spin-drier two years later. By the end of the 1960s I had graduated to a twin-tub and eventually I became the owner of an automatic washing machine. At first I was rather concerned about the waste of water but soon forgot my worries when I realised how convenient and effortless this method of washing was compared with the way things were in my mother's day.'

Shopping and Callers to the Door

Shopping was an event to be savoured, with personal attention in most shops and plenty of time to catch up on gossip! Many goods were brought to our doors, including fresh milk, groceries, bread and meat, and on Sunday afternoon the muffin man might be heard in the street.

◼ Saturday Shopping ◼

'At 72 I can look back and remember so many things about my younger days. Take shopping, for instance. My mother would take us to the main road late evening on Saturday, the goods were much cheaper then. First to the butcher's, where a beautiful smell would greet us. Long oblong trays were spread along the counter, one filled with faggots in gravy. These were cut into squares and put into basins which the customer would bring along with her. Another tray held saveloys, hundreds of them, all gleaming red; next to that was a big sort of vat filled with pease pudding, all golden hot. We were allowed to have one saveloy each with a spoonful of pease pudding as a special treat. My mother would buy cheap cuts of meat such as mutton, and with a large bag of cheap vegetables it was made into a huge stew which would last us for days. Then into the grocers. A marble slab would have a big block of margarine on it; squares were cut from the block by a pair of wooden blades, it was weighed and then patted into shape, either square or round, then it was wrapped.'

◼ Shopping in Wealdstone 1934 ◼

'Apart from the butcher's fat cut around a kidney and rendered down, and that from home made dripping from Sunday's joint, there were just three sorts of fat – lard and margarine for cooking, and butter for spreading. Mother economised by mixing margarine with butter. These stood on separate mounds on Sainsbury's marble counters in their two Wealdstone shops which had prettily tiled walls. Assistants skilfully used two wooden pats, patted out the precise quarity, usually whole, half or quarter of a pound, onto greaseproof paper, first laid on the scales, then an odd piece was added, or removed, until the two scales, one with weights, balanced.

Sugar was often weighed elsewhere into blue "sugar paper" tube-shaped bags, also tea and coffee, but this went into conical shapes formed by rolling a square paper, tucking up the pointed end and twice turning over the open end. Spices and pepper went into smaller squares. Salt was supplied in large brick-shaped fourpenny blocks which were broken down at home. It was often used for preserving sliced runner beans.

Biscuits were also sold loose, from tins, and weighed into paper bags, but good quality broken biscuits were a cheaper buy, often just one penny per paper bag in Woolworths. Nothing there cost over sixpence, eg a glass fruit dish was 2d and the larger fruit bowls 6d – so a complete set of six dishes and bowl was 1s 6d. Mine subsequently survived intact when we had a direct hit with four bombs at Hockerill College in 1940.

In between the two Sainsbury's were several useful shops. The corn merchant was unique, pet and cattle food could be purchased in large sacks and smaller quantities were served from large open top bins. Occasionally there was a suspicion that perhaps mice may have made nightly visits!

Opposite, near to the Harrow and Wealdstone station there was a button shop. There stored in numerous open topped boxes were countless buttons; with much sorting, and not a little patience, the exact number required could always be found. Smaller buttons or odd ones often cost about six for one penny. Larger buttons could be made into attractive brooches or pendants. Sometimes belt buckles were discovered and even the most attractive cost less then 2d, and there was braiding too.

Stays and whale-boned garments designed "to pull a lady in" were displayed in Thomas's draper's shop windows, together

PURE WOOL UNDERWEAR

Winter weight, made in England. Vests with long or short sleeves; ankle length Pants. Sizes 34 to 40 in. SPECIAL PRICE per Garment **6/11**

WINTER Dressing Gown

In plain Grey, Brown, Fawn, and Lovat, trimmed and corded in harmonising effects. All sizes up to 44 in. chest. SPECIAL PRICE **35/-**

with lisle stockings, suspenders, navy bloomers and flannelette nightwear. There were liberty bodices for those younger, and always long black wool stockings held up by garters under gym slips. There was also a camisole that wrapped across the breasts, designed, I suppose, to make them less conspicuous! Inside this shop had huge wooden counters with a chair for the customer. After selecting a purchase, the money and bill disappeared in a container that, as a rope was pulled downwards, travelled overhead. After a while it reappeared, with a loud plop, from a tube behind the assistant who then opened the container and handed the bill, change, and often also a packet of pins or safety pins instead of the farthing which should have been included. Most prices were, say, 1s 11¾d. My mother did not buy her boned under-garments from there because we had a relative who was an agent for Spirella corsets and she used to visit from time to time. They were quite expensive, being made to measure, and so these were not for me, for which after seeing Mother tightly laced in I was very thankful.'

▣ THE MUFFIN MAN ▣

'My memories of my childhood in Ponders End, Enfield include winter Sunday afternoons when the muffin man came round the streets ringing his bell and carrying a tray of fresh muffins on his head. We children waited at the gate in anticipation. The muffins were toasted over the open fire in the parlour. This was our Sunday treat. We also used to have a man with a barrow on which he had winkles, shrimps and cockles for sale.'

▣ THE CAT'S MEAT MAN ▣

'During the 1930s the cat's meat man used to push through our letter box in Southall, once a week, several chunks of cooked meat on a skewer. The cat knew exactly when it would plonk on to the front door mat and would take possession should we not be on hand to rescue it and put it into the outdoor meat safe for another day.'

▣ COAL AND SOOT ▣

'Before the war, tradesmen came to the door delivering milk, bread and meat each weekday. The coalman came regularly and emptied his sacks into the coal cellar while we watched to see that he had delivered the correct amount of coal. Twice every season the sweep arrived to keep the chimney clean. We children would dash outside into the garden to see the sweep's brush appear above the top of the chimneypot. Occasionally the chimney would catch fire and hot cinders would rain down into the open grate. A really good chimney on fire would merit a visit by the fire brigade, but this never happened at our house!'

⬙ THE HANDY STORES ⬙

'Farm Road, Staines, was a cul-de-sac at the end of Witheygate Avenue, which is off the Worple Road. It was in Worple Road that my aunt had her shop, "The Handy Stores". I loved my Auntie Dorrie and that shop, except at times when, quite often on my arrival home from school, before I got a foot in the door, my mother would say, "Pop up to Auntie's and get me five Weights or Woodbines." I hated those little paper packets of cigarettes, especially as I used to quite often have to say, "Mum says could you put them on the slate?"

Auntie was lovely to look at and to be with. She lived on the premises and there was a long passage and her sitting room between the back of her bungalow and the shop. A bell jangled loudly on its spring when one opened the door, and Auntie always came running along the passage, her high heels tap-tapping on the lino, and there was always her lovely smile to greet you.

I remember brass scales swinging on long chains with brass weights of different sizes in piles on the marble base. Large stone jars filled with vinegar had little taps on the side, and if Auntie wasn't too busy she would let me fill a bottle myself, under her supervision.

Auntie could make a paper cone as quick as a flash! These would be filled with all manner of dried goods, soda crystals, powder, sugar, dried peas, beans, lentils, rice and sweets. There was another scale with cast iron base and weights and a flat marble top on which cheese was weighed, cut with wire from a whole cheese, and butter that was cut and shaped between wooden pats before being wrapped in greaseproof paper.

Along one side of the long shop, behind a big wooden counter, were rows of wooden shelves. On the lower shelves stood tall tins of tobacco with names like Light Shag, Dark Shark and Plug on them. The Plug would be cut with a sharp knife, weighed and put into a sort of envelope-shaped bag and Shag was sold by weight too. There were smaller square tins of different colours, this was cigarette tobacco, and neatly stacked packets of Rizla cigarette papers to roll it in. Beside the hated Weights and Woodbines were attractive packets of cigarettes which I thought would be much nicer to smoke, with names like Black Cat, Craven A, De Reske and Du Maurier.

On higher shelves were lots of large jars of sweets (more tempting than today's plastic packets) – pear drops, cough candy, golden humbugs, fat sherbet lemons, raspberries and blackberries, liquorice shoelaces and aniseed balls which one sucked down to the little black seed in the centre, and pretty Phul-Nana cachous, though I think it was the label that attracted me more than the powdery scented flavour.

On Boat Race day Auntie sold little celluloid dolls dressed in feathers of Cambridge or Oxford blue. They had a safety pin in their back. I wore my Cambridge doll for weeks after, even if they lost the race.'

▣ THE SHOPPING REMINDER ▣

'When in 1934 we moved into a newly built house in Harrow Weald the kitchen cabinet had, and still has, a label declaring: "A Hygena Cabinet Brings Joy To The Home". This headed a shopping reminder of 72 items, small flaps being flipped over to indicate those needed. Ammonia, Blue Disinfectant, Plate Powder, Polish (usually Mansion), Spirits, Starch, Soda, Turpentine and Vim were for household cleaning. Whiting was not a species of fish but a cardboard box containing a white block and damp sponge used for almost daily cleaning of white canvas gym shoes.

Shepperton village shops between the wars.

Dentifrice (Gibbs) was in a round flat tin, often accompanied by adverts with fairies cleaning ivory castles – teeth. The alternative was soot from the chimney, or salt. Yes, the toothbrush really was just first rubbed inside the chimney.

Firewood was needed to start off the coal fire, but it was quite usual to chop one's own from old boxes in which groceries may have been delivered. Corn was bought to feed poultry often kept in hen houses in the back garden. Cornflour was used for blancmange, usually served with jelly.

Soups were usually home-made, but Symingtons sold a tomato soup in powder form in a small packet. Jam was usually in jars. These were rinsed and taken back to the shop for a penny or halfpenny refund. Like milk bottles they were recycled, but sometimes "borrowed" for home-made jam.

Milk, delivered on the doorstep, was in a wide necked glass bottle sealed by a cardboard disc, usually with a lift up tab, pressed into the top. Before pouring care had to be taken that there was no dust on the rim as this could be poured with the milk. Coffee was either Camp Essence poured from a bottle to be mixed with hot water, or expensive ground and only served on very special occasions.

Suet was cut by the butcher from around a kidney and sold for very few pence. It was then rendered down and used for cooking meat but "bread and dripping" was a favourite winter treat.

Bath salts or bath cubes are interesting omissions from the list. Reckitts used to have adverts of "Mary Smith" (or such like) entering a bath with a cube, and "Lady Maria Smyth, Duchess of..." coming out!'

◙ SHOPS IN HARROW WEALD ◙

'Throughout Middlesex there must have been local groups of shopkeepers who together provided daily needs for surrounding housewives. For young mothers, shopping meant wheeling children in cumbersome perambulators or non-folding pushchairs. It was essential to have everyday commodities near at home.

Few had cars, rather more had bicycles, but most walked and then went by bus and/or tube. It was a red letter day when a number 18 bus service went from Wealdstone, up Locket Road, over Belmont Circle and via Cannons Park station to Edgware, in about 1938.

In the mid 1930s, Kenton Lane was still narrow with high hedgerows and the College Hill Road end of Bishops Ken was still a footpath alongside a field. On its corner with Kenton Lane was The Cabin, a hut with just one counter inside. People gathered there about four o'clock to buy the daily evening edition of *The Star*. Also sold were daily newspapers such as the *Daily Herald, Daily Mirror* and some magazines such as *Woman's Weekly, Titbits* and *Popular Gardening*. On a side shelf there were boxes of non-safety matches (that easily ignited and could explode, burning the hand), some more expensive boxes of safety matches and the more elegant, longer Swan Vestas. There were hairgrips, hair nets, pipe cleaners, and packs of potatoes were also sold. Gradually gales caused this wooden shack to disintegrate and, as Rose Farm flats were being built, the owner moved into Hodge's newspaper and sweet business opposite.

Normally, when bought, freshly baked bread was partially swathed in a flimsy piece of white tissue paper. I remember the dairy first selling a large tin loaf completely wrapped in a wax-like paper on which were printed details of a competition – complete with no more than ten words: "I like Neville's wrapped bread because…" My "it is easier to carry home without a shopping basket" won ten shillings and an invitation for my parents and me to tour their bakery at Acton. There we met the other prize winners – a younger girl had won the first prize (£2). Each family went home with a bag of goodies. Wrapped bread tended to "sweat", possibly still steaming when wrapped. I suspect that the factory may have been bombed during the war, so causing the demise of Neville's bread.

Next to the dairy was the chemist's with a double front with lovely wooden bow windows. Miss Brown was a fully qualified chemist and apart from managing the dispensary she weighed the babies and was always ready with advice, often prescribing medicines that she made up and so often saving doctor's fees. Mothers could safely leave their prams outside the shop, and swapped information and help with problems and got to know one another. Shopping was a friendly experience. Here there was a penny library where readers could borrow books weekly. Once a returned book had a wad of notes used as a bookmark. Since everybody knew each other it was easy to return the money to the rightful owner when she was next in the shop. At the back Miss Brown's married sister ran the post office which provided all available services.

Next door was Mr Percy's greengrocer's selling high quality produce. Oranges, lemons and sometimes apples came individually wrapped in tissue with designs indicating their origin. I filled an album with many different wrappers collected for a geography competition. Mr Percy installed a large refrigerated chest and sold Smedley's frozen peas. Later (1952) he had frozen fish which was rock hard and had to be thawed under running cold water before it could be cooked.

The cobbler always kept our leather shoes well heeled and with soles that ensured that they lasted. The ladies in the wool shop were always interested and ready with advice about knitting patterns.

The Co-op was the largest central store and, apart from groceries, supplied paraffin much needed for stoves in winter time. Families paid one shilling for a share book and a check was made out in duplicate, using carbon paper, with the share number (ours was 24114) for all purchases. These were collected together and at the end of each quarter members received notification of their "Divi". The dividends, possibly sixpence in the pound, were entered in the book from which withdrawals, and deposits, could be made. Since the Co-op had branches that sold furniture and similar major items, and catered for weddings and funerals, the "divi" provided a valuable extra income.

The manager usually made up orders which were delivered by an errand boy with a bicycle after school and at no extra charge, it was part of the service. Bacon was selected from sides on show and cut by the manager to a required thickness. It was wrapped in thick white kitchen paper. Customers always carried shopping bags. Eggs were put into paper bags, but most items went unwrapped into customers' own bags. Shareholders of the Co-op attended annual meetings at which they could offer suggestions and discuss complaints about *their* shops.

At the far end was the barber who first cut my long hair when in 1939 I was going to college. It was some years later that he acquired a lady assistant in a separate section but, if needed, hair was still shampooed in the "barber's". Usually it was done at home beforehand.

All the shops closed on Wednesday and Saturday afternoons and on Sundays. Rose Farm would always sell fresh cream on a Sunday morning provided the customer had a jug!

Our milkman delivered every day, as did the postman twice, except only once on Sundays and Christmas Day.'

◙ JUST AROUND THE CORNER IN SOUTHALL ◙

'I often had to go shopping for Mum, in the 1940s, down the main road in Southall. She used to be a member of the Co-op (I can still remember her "divi" number). The Co-op shop for groceries was just before the town hall on the north side of the Uxbridge Road, and was a long narrowish shop. There were counters down each side of the central concourse with lady assistants behind each section. I used to start at the bacon counter on the right-hand side (six rashers of unsmoked back) and work my way right down to the end and back up the other side. The wonder of it was that at each counter the lady would recognise me, and they knew Mum's shopping list (which I always carried with me – written out carefully in counter order) almost as well as my mother. Of course, rationing made the weekly list pretty well standard with few variations. I had my favourites among the assistants; the grey haired lady behind the bacon

Out shopping in Uxbridge in 1950.

counter was particularly nice, and most of them treated me really "grown up" so I used to enjoy shopping on my own for Mum.

We had our meat from Biggs the butcher's, the newspapers from Thompson's the paper shop, the fruit (when available) and vegetables from the greengrocer, all "just around the corner".

Occasional visits were made by bus to the "big" Co-op in Hounslow (120 bus to Bell Corner), and the Co-op tailor and shoe shop over "The Green", Southall, which was in fact at the beginning of King Street by the old Dominion cinema.'

▣ CHISWICK HIGH ROAD ▣

'Chiswick High Road used to be very noisy and lively on Saturday afternoons. This was the time many of us with full time jobs had to shop for our families. The pavements were crowded, the shops had stalls brightly lit, and much of the noise came from the butchers who stood at their doors shouting to encourage people to buy the meat they were selling at knock-down prices before the weekend. Many of us waited until the last ten minutes or so to get our meat. Some of the shops had beautiful pictures of sheep and cows in blue and white tiles on their walls. All these have gone now.'

◈ DELIVERIES IN THE 1960S ◈

'When we came to live in Ponders End in 1960 gas was still in use to light our little cul de sac. The baker delivered bread to the door with a great choice of loaves. If I phoned the butcher in the early morning his wife would bring the day's meat for dinner. We would have a little chat to enquire as to everyone's well being.'

◈ THE WEEKLY BUDGET IN 1965 ◈

'A mother of three young children recorded her weekly housekeeping expenses in 1965:

	£	s	d
Groceries	3	10	0
Meat and fish	2	0	0
Fruit and vegetables	1	0	0
Milk	1	1	0
Bread		10	0
Children's clothes	1	5	0
Hair cutting		4	0
Nursery school		5	0
Chemist and sundries		10	0

This gave a total expenditure of £10 5s. Family allowance came to 18s, so her outgoings were £9 7s a week.'

FROM THE CRADLE TO THE GRAVE

We were much more likely to have our babies at home, to be married from home and to die in our home in the past.

▨ GETTING WED IN 1948 ▨

'I remember my younger brother's wedding day as if it was yesterday, in fact it took place on 24th July 1948 at St Anslem's church in Hayes. He lived at number 98 Birchway and his bride lived across the road at number 97, so all the neighbours were involved.

Food was still on rationing, and as we were having the reception at our house, all the neighbours had been chipping in for weeks with sugar, butter, dried fruit that they had managed to get hold of although it was still in short supply, fresh eggs, milk and, on the week of the actual wedding, part of their cheese ration and cooked meats for sandwiches. Some of them even made cakes, jellies and trifles and brought them along to the house. They even gave my mother part of their very precious tea ration that they had saved up. Neighbours in those days were very friendly and helped each other when they could.

The bride, like all young girls, had set her heart on a white wedding with bridesmaids, but clothing coupons were still in use. A girl that she worked with at Nestlé's had recently been married and she lent her the long white satin dress and all the accessories, but it was not so easy getting bridesmaids' dresses. Here her father came to the rescue.

Her father, and older sister, worked for the Great Western Railway at Paddington station in the goods department. He drove a large cart with a shire horse and delivered goods to the East End of London where the rag trade operated. When he explained to the shop people what was happening it was arranged that the bride, her father and two bridesmaids go to

London one Saturday morning and visit one of their shops. This we did and chose two identical dresses that, after much discussion, the bridesmaids had agreed on. When it came time to pay and hand over the necessary clothing coupons her father went to the back of the shop with the owner and we heard later that, for every clothing coupon needed for the dresses, instead he had paid an extra amount on the bill. I guess this was what was known at the time as the "black market"! To be economical we chose dresses with summer patterns on them, and I wore mine for several years afterwards.

The sun was shining and at the church my brother and his best man looked very splendid in their "demob" suits. The church was packed with all the relations, friends and neighbours who had come along. My mother panicked, would she have enough food for everyone?

She need not have worried because after the reception when the bride and groom had left for their honeymoon in Bude, there was plenty of food left over and this was divided up amongst the neighbours who had so kindly helped to provide it all.'

▣ FACTS ABOUT MIDWIVES ▣

'In 1938 as a ten year old living in Ruislip Manor I had heard of midwives but, as an only child, I had never seen one close up so when one day my mother casually let drop that Mrs Foxwell who lived next door was expecting a baby and that a midwife would be calling there I was agog to see one in person.

Disappointingly, she looked like any other woman I had ever seen, even to the extent of wearing a hat, though this one was slightly different in that it looked like an upturned saucepan without a handle and was deep blue in colour. What did make her different, however, was that she arrived in a car! Cars were not a common sight in Whitby Road at this time and especially driven by a woman.

The midwife, no doubt in her haste, parked her beautiful brown and gleaming Ruby some three feet away from the kerb before rushing into Mrs Foxwell's. So far I had discovered three facts about midwives: they wore funny hats, they drove motor cars and they carried black bags, and it was whilst I pondered over these clues that I became aware of three very large steamrollers slowly and majestically trundling up the road towards me; was there some connection I wondered? Surely not.

Obviously there wasn't because the first two, in close line astern, came abreast and noisily passed by, but the third, some distance behind did not. Its driver was in deep and shouted conversation with somebody walking alongside him on his right and so failed to spot the midwife's car. The resulting collision was both loud and destructive and all in wonderful slow motion. The impact slewed the little car around and propelled it several yards up the road, the noise of this and the yells of the driver and his colleague were sufficiently loud to bring the midwife rushing out from next door.

I then discovered a further means of identifying one of these mysterious creatures; for, if this one was typical, they were jolly good at swearing!'

◈ HAVING BABIES AT HOME ◈

'Three of my babies were born at home between 1947 and 1953, following a very difficult protracted hospital birth for my first baby. I had attended ante-natal clinic all though my pregnancies, with advantages of regular check-ups and the "perks" of free cod liver oil, orange juice and Colacts, a chocolate drink which was quite enjoyable and a supplement containing vitamins, etc. I also visited my family doctor who was to be present at the birth, though the midwives, a jolly competent and efficient band of "girls" were proud of being independent and able to cope with any eventuality.

About a month before the infant was due a large parcel was delivered by a midwife to the house and stored on top of the wardrobe, out of the way. This contained sterile articles to be used by the midwife at the birth, including a large waterproof bedcovering which could be disposed of neatly and efficiently. My babies all started to arrive in the early hours, so it meant staying awake and timing contractions till five minute intervals – when "Dad" went to the phone on the corner to call the midwife. Not so bad if one had had experience before, but a bit daunting wondering if she would make it in time! The doctor was also called, and the information passed on. I was lucky enough to have the babies arrive before the children stirred and they were awakened with the exciting news that a new baby had arrived while they were asleep.

The Moses basket had been arranged ready for its new occupant, and Dad had been posted downstairs, standing by the boiler and kettle for that wonderful cup of tea, which tasted like nectar. In this way the family felt part of the whole operation. The nurses continued to visit for about ten days to a fortnight. I certainly wasn't expected to be on my feet straight away; my doctor said, "Try to rest as much as possible, you won't get much after that for some while!"'

'Our first child was born in Queen Charlotte's Maternity Hospital in Hammersmith but when the second was expected in 1960, I was not allowed to book a hospital place as we had a three bedroomed house, and was forced to give birth at home.

I was visited throughout the pregnancy by a very pleasant young midwife in whom I had the utmost confidence but when the time came, she was off duty and a very elderly nurse arrived and I thought she was old enough to be retired. Her first words were, "Bring some bricks up into the bedroom" – my husband and I looked at her in amazement, we thought it was certainly no time to take up bricklaying! However, she explained these were needed to raise the bed. After an initial examination, she left me and went downstairs and chatted with my husband and I had to bang on the floor to get her to return and attend to me! After providing the compulsory hot water, my husband sat on the stairs throughout – husbands were definitely not invited to view the intimate procedure, and we were rewarded by the birth of a lovely baby girl.

We subsequently had another son in 1966 in Central Middlesex Hospital as the rules on home births had been reversed.'

◼ NURSED AT HOME ◼

'When my brother had scarlet fever he was nursed at home with a sheet hung over the bedroom door, its bottom in a bowl of Lysol.

When a neighbour was very ill, straw was scattered over the road to quieten the noise of horses' hooves.'

◼ CALL THE NEIGHBOUR ◼

'As as child I lived at Stanwell Moor, we were only a small village, where everybody knew everyone else. We walked to school, which was just over a mile, to Stanwell village. I am talking about the 1930s, there was not a lot of money about. If you needed a doctor you had to pay, so before you saw your doctor you called your neighbour. In our case it was Mrs Salter next door, her family were older than us, so be it a sore throat, a rash or a headache, even a stomach pain, she would with Mother's help diagnose your complaint, then they would decide on a cure. Oh dear, that would be worse than the illness. Nobody ever feigned illness to escape school, I can tell you.'

◼ DOCTORS AND DENTISTS ◼

'In the late 1930s I started to have a lot of ear, nose and throat problems and was constantly being taken to the doctor. Dr Elven held his surgery at his home on the Kingston Road, Staines. I was lucky because I liked going to him, his house was big and had lovely soft carpets and shiny tables and chairs.

He had a round smiley face, and wore glasses. He always made me laugh, though I didn't like it when he pushed shiny tools in my ears. Eventually it was decided to remove my tonsils and adenoids and I was admitted to Staines Cottage Hospital which was almost opposite the doctor's house.

I remember I was not in the least worried about going into hospital, I was made a great fuss of and the nurses were always making me glasses of sherbet which I loved. One of them would dance me around the wards singing to me.

I remember very clearly having a rubber cap put on my head and long thick white woollen socks put on my feet. I was carried into theatre by a nurse and laid on a table covered in white sheets, then a little white muslin mask was held over my nose and mouth and I can remember the smell of ether to this day.

When I woke I was given only jellies and ice cream for several days, and when the day came for me to go home I cried buckets of tears.

My first encounter with the dentist in 1938 was not such a happy experience as the doctor and hospital. It was at the school dental clinic housed in a large wooden hut situated at the back of Kingston Road School, Staines, although I think I was still a pupil at Wyatt Road School at this time, where they probably did not have a clinic.

On opening the door of the hut you were in an oblong room and at the far end was a door leading into the dentist's surgery. To the left was a row of chairs to sit on while waiting to enter the surgery, on the right side of the room was a circle of chairs. Some of these were already occupied by children who had been into the surgery, and to my horror these children, some in tears, were bending over hand-held bowls with water in, into which they were spitting blood.

This sight absolutely terrified me and when my turn came I had to be held down in the chair while the gas mask, as it was called, was held over my face. After the horrid deed was done I too was ushered into a chair with my little bowl of water to spit blood into.

Wyatt Road school facilities were very different when my son, Clifford, went there in 1957.'

CHILDHOOD & SCHOOLDAYS

CHILDHOOD DAYS

The freedom to roam the fields and woods of the countryside, the delights of life on the river or around the village green – just some of the memories of childhood

◼ CENTRED ON THE VILLAGE GREEN AT WEST DRAYTON ◼

'Most of my memories of the 1920s centre on the village green in West Drayton which is still as it was then except for a few changes. It was the venue for the maypole on May Day and a large bonfire on 5th November, but best of all were the two weeks in the summer when Beeches Fair visited us. What fun it was to chase each other in and out of the stalls with the odd shout from the owners. I think we were all fascinated by watching the steam engine working the lights and music for the merry-go-round, the cost of which was 2d a ride.

During Ascot Week horse-drawn brakes would leave the pubs full of merry folks for the yearly outing to the races. In the late afternoon we children would listen for the approach home and as soon as we could hear the singing we would run as far as Thorney to greet them knowing that pennies would be thrown out for us to gather.

Just off the green was Money Lane where I was born. It was a lovely country lane with a stream running by the road where at the appropriate time we would paddle and fish. Sadly, this no longer exists.

Through the seasons we would skip, play hopscotch, bowl our hoops, whip tops and play "fag cards". All this activity would take place in the road as no cars ever came our way.

School was at the old church school where now stands the library. There were two classrooms heated by one huge coal-fired stove. During the summer months we would go to Providence Road school in Yiewsley once a week to learn how to launder

June Hill in 1930, an Uxbridge girl.

and iron clothes: winter months we would go to learn cooking. All this before we were ten years old.'

▣ LIFE ON THE THAMES ▣

'I have lived in Shepperton all my life (73 years). My father, Russell Rosewell, had a boating business on the Thames. We lived nearby. He spent long hours looking after the boats which were mostly punts and skiffs. They were kept on the Thames near his family home. Each day, the cushions had to be put in the boats; these were stored in the house. The boats were let to local people by the hour or half hour. I remember taking out rowing boats myself.

We were all taught to swim at an early age. My father taught us by holding us out on a piece of webbing attached to a punt pole. It was a case of sink or swim! I am very glad I learnt to swim as I was then able to swim in the Thames on my own, or with family and friends.

We lived near Walton Bridge and used to go for a swim with our costumes on under our coats. Many times I have swum across the river and back again. Later, we would swim from a bathing station nearby, where we could dry ourselves and change our clothes.

My days at the local council school were very happy. We walked there about a mile away, along footpaths across farm fields. We took a packed lunch. Small bottles of milk were delivered to the school, these were put inside the fireguard around the open fire and the metal tops used to lift as the milk got warm, delicious on a cold winter's day. We were allowed out early if the days were dark or foggy, to get home safely; some days we were told not to use the footpaths as Old Bill Sikes was about!'

▣ CHORES TO DO ▣

'When I was a child in the late 1930s we had our regular tasks to do around the home. My favourite was blackleading the kitchen range with Zeebo; if I failed to get this job I had to be content with the firegrates in the two living rooms. I also liked clearing out the ashes and laying the fires ready for use – the front room was mainly only used when we had visitors and on Sunday. I was sent shopping as Uxbridge had many small grocers, butchers, bakers and greengrocers, all within easy reach and without the hazard of traffic. I disliked the butcher, though, because he called me "sweetheart" which I found embarrassing so I forgot what I had gone for! Other chores I had to do included polishing furniture, the lino and shoes; washing and drying dishes; making beds; and, my most loathed job, cleaning cutlery.'

▣ A VAST EXPANSE OF FIELDS ▣

'My memories of Middlesex go back to 1936. I was nearly six years old, and we had moved from Dorchester in Dorset to Staines. We were the first family to take up residence in a newly built row of houses, that stood in a vast expanse of fields and farmland, giving rise to the name "Farm Road".

My mother and father had chosen the end house at the far end of the road adjacent to the farm, and in the early days it was a frequent occurrence to have cows, horses, ducks and chickens wandering in the back garden, that is until Father, a keen gardener, started to cultivate the ground, then the farmer, Mr Worsfold, a nice man who sadly died of a wasp sting, put up a strong fence.

The next family to arrive were Welsh and they chose the house at the other end of the road. Mrs Huxtable was a kind person, she always came to our house whenever there was a wedding, christening or funeral to make the tea, so that it was ready to be poured into the best teacups as soon as family and guests arrived back from the church.

For a time my youngest brother and I were able to walk across open fields and cross a stream by walking along a fallen tree to our infants' school in Wyatt Road. It wasn't very long before other houses and bungalows were built around us, though there were still open fields at the back and down Commercial Lane (now Road), also much of Worple Road was still open land. House building stopped with the outbreak of war in 1939.'

▣ THE SUNDAY AFTERNOON WALK ▣

'One of my strongest memories of childhood years in the 1930s was the "Sunday Afternoon Walk". My sister and I, who always walked together a few paces ahead of our parents, wore identical powder blue coats, black patent shoes, fastened with one button, and white socks. Father wore his best suit, complete with waistcoat and pocket watch, bowler hat and walking stick. I cannot remember Mother's outfit, but I have no doubt it was equally unsuitable for walking, compared to today's fashions. On the way home, my sister and I would enliven the walk by awarding points, up to ten, for the best front gardens viewed in passing.

On returning home, it was our job to make toast for tea by the heat from a coal fire, using a long-handled toasting fork. The pleasure obtained from this activity far outweighed the discomfort felt from scorching cheeks and hands, as we bent over the fire. Rescuing the odd slice of toast from the flames where it had slipped from the fork only increased the excitement.

If there were no doilies available for the cake plates, my sister and I would make our own by cutting circles of paper, folding them in half repeatedly, and then snipping out various shapes from the folded edges. They must have been very crude, but we thought they were wonderful.'

▣ LIVING WITH GRANDMA ▣

'Having lost my mother when I was five years old, I spent the next four years living with various people, two of whom were my grandparents in Southall. My grandmother suffered very badly with osteoarthritis and I used to "help" her do various jobs around the house.

Whilst in her care, a few amusing things come to mind. I was a sickly child with constant chest infections, and was made to wear a liberty bodice inside which was placed a large piece of "thermogene wool", the fumes from which made my eyes run and I was continually sneezing at school! I was also given Virol each day (which I liked) and Scotts Emulsion (which I hated), as well as regular doses of cod liver oil and syrup of figs! They had an outside toilet and three steps to go down to the garden and a few times I only just made it! I remember the toilet had a huge wooden seat that stretched from wall to wall and it was my job to tear newspaper into squares and thread a piece of string in one corner – this was toilet paper.

Another job I was given was to cut up a block of salt for the water softener, for although it was the early 1940s, my Gran actually had a washing machine – a big green round one, with rubber rollers, in which she put "softened" water and then flaked bar of Lifebuoy soap (also my job to cut up the soap). When the washing was done I had to turn the handle of the large wringer, with wooden rollers (in the garden).

They had a huge clock on the wall in the dining room with long pendulums which swung from side to side, which my grandfather used to pull down once a day (I have hated "ticking clocks" ever since). He also had a long glass case in the hall in which was a massive pike, caught by himself in his younger days – he founded the "Southall Piscatorial Society".

One thing I used to really enjoy was playing on their pianola in which were paper rolls of music, with holes to make the notes. All I had to do was push the pedals with my feet – I used to think I was so clever, being able to play *Red Sails in the Sunset* all by myself. I must have driven them mad, as this was my favourite tune and was played over and over.'

▣ FRESH AIR IN ISLEWORTH ▣

'I went to an Open Air School in Isleworth, where I would have breakfast on arrival. We had to have a sleep on camp beds after dinner. The classrooms and activity hall had floor to ceiling windows which always seemed to be opened, lots of lessons were taken outside and I remember we also did lots of gardening. This was in 1948 when I was ten.

Before we went to Guide camp we had head inspection, any girl having lice would not be allowed to go. Friday night was bath and hair washing in the tin bath. Mum would sit with a black apron on her lap and I would have to kneel in front of her and she would comb our hair checking for head lice; if found our hair would be washed with black soap.

Maltesers were the first sweets I remember buying when sweets came off ration. Friday night I would be given 1s 6d pocket money and a two ounce sweet coupon. I would buy the smallest sweets I could to make them last; we had a lovely corner shop that sold most things including penny bags of crisps and broken biscuits.'

GAMES AND TREATS

We got little, if any, pocket money and our games were usually cheaply arranged. They followed the seasons and we were able to see the streets as our playground with so little motor traffic to bother us.

◈ HAPPY DAYS BEFORE THE FIRST WORLD WAR ◈

'When we were small we girls found the greatest pleasure in our dolls, some were really lovely and have been treasured as collector's pieces. My sister and I had a large dolls' house with which we spent may happy hours. It had an upstairs and a downstairs, with a staircase. I think the kitchen gave us the greatest fun with all the cooking utensils, etc. Its final destination was an orphanage in Enfield.

The outdoor games were seasonal. One of the favourites was the hoop; the boys' hoops were made of iron which were propelled by an iron skimmer, the girls had wooden hoops. The size was a kind of status symbol, the largest being the most longed for. We each had our nail in the shed on which to hang our hoop. What is really almost unbelievable in this different world is that we could bowl our hoops down the middle of the road, there was so little traffic. Then came skipping, ball games of great variety, marbles, five stones, etc, but another favourite was the spinning top, I mean the peg-top, around which boys wound cord then released it and pitched it onto the ground, whipping it to keep it going. The girls' top was lighter and small being made of boxwood and was called "Boxer". In bad weather we, in our family, were allowed a special section of the kitchen floor on which to play tops.

In the school playground we played rather complicated singing games which I think had some historical associations, but my memory fails me here! Our great love was learning to play tennis and taking part in the school tournament. We were also taught hockey.

Many of the indoor games have survived, ludo, snakes and ladders, pit, snap, tiddly winks, several card games and many more.

Birthday and particularly Christmas parties were highlights. Summer birthdays were celebrated out of doors, with tea under the trees followed by games in the orchard. Christmas parties were rather different, where we played, among others, Twirl the Trencher, a fast moving game, Come and Sit on my Chair, Consequences, Winking (a rather cheeky game this) and charades. But what we most enjoyed was our magic lantern, when a sheet was pinned to the wall, a screen put in front of the fire and the lamp taken out. The children, there were usually about ten of us, sat on the floor. My father put through the slides, all coloured. He made the stars twinkle as we sang *Twinkle, Twinkle Little Star*, and a seesaw moved up and down, and many others. I remember some lovely pictures of London.

I am talking now of the days when there were no cinemas or other forms of public entertainment. The local church choir put on concerts, inviting well-known celebrities to take part. These were very popular, attracting good attendances. Some years after the magic lantern period, our private entertainment was the musical evenings when we, and friends, gathered around the piano and sang what are now called the old ballads – we lifted the rafters!

Many a jolly afternoon was spent dancing "the light fantastic" at the tea dances which were held in a large reception room at the local restaurant. At one shilling per head they were good money-spinners and enabled the Women's Institute to buy curtains for the stage at our hall.

As the four young people of our family grew older we became enthusiastic walkers, exploring the surrounding country. Ten minutes' walk brought us to the river Lea where we were always interested in watching the barges being negotiated through the lock gates. At this boundary point between Middlesex and Essex we passed through a toll gate kept by a keeper with a wooden leg; the toll we paid was one penny.

This was the road to Epping Forest, a favourite walk this, no houses but on one side, since 1912, was the George V Reservoir, which was opened by the King and Queen Mary. I remember seeing them pass by our house on their way, to cheers from the people. At the beginning of the First World War a munitions factory was built nearby, thus spoiling the country atmosphere. However, before that happened, we had many happy days in the forest, picnics under the large, spreading trees, walking and boating on the lake, Connaught Water. It was to Epping Forest that hundreds of trippers went on bank holidays. They travelled in brakes drawn by two or four horses; a man sitting beside the driver blew a cornet, playing all the popular songs.

On our walks along the country lanes on summer evenings, we sometimes caught the tiny sparks of light from glowworms in the hedges.'

◼ TEN TERRIBLE TESTS ◼

'Aspiring members to "Our Gang" had to pass Ten Terrible Tests, each of which would have made our mothers' hair go grey overnight if they had known. I recall some of them – playing chicken across the railway line, balancing round the rim of a sunken barge at the old gravel pits around the Stanwell area, and similar dare-devil acts.

One bitterly cold day, my brother, aged seven, tried one test which was to pole-vault across the Grand Union Canal at Yiewsley. He had a good run-up along the towpath, hurled himself into space, firmly planting his pole in the canal centre and gracefully slid down into the water. We got him out, a non-swimmer at that time, stripped him, except for his knitted tie which had shrunk, wrapped him in our coats and then ran up and down the tow path with his clothes held aloft, fondly imagining we could dry them and Mum would never know.

Eventually when he was blue with cold and we were exhausted, we decided to face the music. An aunt was having tea with Mum, and whilst the latter ran to draw a hot bath my aunt tried to get the shrunken tie off. She tugged and pulled until she nearly strangled the poor child, but his ordeal was not yet over. Aunt gave up the struggle, seized a pair of scissors and advanced. Heaven knows what he thought was about to happen, but with a loud yell he tore upstairs and was found cowering under his bed.

In all the excitement, my part and my punishment were forgotten until Dad came home, but that is another story…'

◙ POCKET MONEY ◙

'In the late 1930s I was a pupil at Harrow county school. I had a florin (two shillings) pocket money each week. Bus journeys took 1s 8d a week at a penny a time as I came home for lunch. I paid a halfpenny for my daily glass of milk, so that was another 2½d gone. We gave another halfpenny for school charities each week, and this left a penny for the Sunday collection. Sometimes I saved a penny by walking home. Fortunately my grandmother put aside threepence a week and when we visited her in Derby she gave me a month's or more pocket money. It went towards a new fountain pen, warm gloves or knitting wool. We never bought books, they were always borrowed from the library.'

✦ A Magical House ✦

'How I envied my friend, who lived in a magical house. You entered through large wooden gates which had a small door cut into them. The ground floor had been a coach house and stable which provided us with a large play area with old mangers and troughs making toys which stretched our imaginations. There were many boxes of junk, including some "dressing up" clothes, wonderful Twenties style dresses, feathers and high heeled shoes. The living accommodation on the first floor was a maze of small rooms with sloping ceilings, uneven floors and higgledy-piggledy windows with tiny panes of glass.

The glory was the garden, very long with lovely hiding places and in the centre was a huge mulberry tree under which we had picnics and dolls' tea parties. The mulberry fruit I can taste now, the black ripe berries full of juice, running down our chins and staining our hands dark red. To children who rarely had sweets it was heaven.

This wonderful house and garden is now covered by several blocks of flats and the mulberry tree was chopped down. The house was situated at the corner of Craven Road, Ealing and St Leonards Road.'

✦ When Northwood was a Village ✦

'It was a long time ago that Northwood was just a village, or so it seems, when boys played marbles along the kerbstones, or struck spinning tops on their way along Green Lane and Rickmansworth Road, or girls bowled their hoops or played hopscotch on their way to school.

After school in those days it was a case of finding your own thing to do. In the better weather we could help at one of the many farms in the area, either looking out for the livestock or helping with haymaking, or if you were lucky to have a grandfather who was a farrier, you could "blow the bellows" in the forge or collect and deliver the horses after shoeing to the owners.

In the winter weather there was skating on the pond (the ice

Beryl Garrett, with her brother and sister, having fun in the 1930s.

always seemed thicker in those days), snow-balling and thoroughly enjoying yourselves, then home to huddle round the coal fire. No central heating when we were youngsters.'

◙ AT PLAY ◙

'During my early years in Staines, before the war really started to change our way of life, it seems to me the sun always shone. We played in the streets, fields and parks or went to "The Lammas" where there was a big swimming pool and a smaller paddling pool, all day in the school holidays or late into the evening after school.

Chalk was much used for drawing on pavements and roads for hopscotch squares, and lines beyond which one dared not step. We played spinning tops with whips, flicking cigarette cards and rolling marbles against the kerbstone or fence, while countless hours were spent skipping over ropes backwards and forwards, clever ones twisting the rope overhead. Rounders and hockey could be played in our street, a cul-de-sac, and I don't remember anyone having a car at that time.

Later at twelve or 13 years old, we had cycles and would cycle to Coopers Hill and back with our pickings of blackberries. We would then erect a stall outside George Diamond's double gates – he was the son of a builder and had all the equipment to erect the stall – there we would sell our pickings for a few pence. We usually spent it on sweets.

Another pastime was putting on amateur variety shows. One boy in our street, Laurie Langford, had a garage, though I don't remember seeing a car in it, and his mother would let us put our shows on there. We got collecting boxes from the cottage hospital and all the money was dropped through the slot as Mums, Dads and kids came to watch us perform. We would proudly deliver it to the hospital next day.'

◙ THE FARM LORRY ◙

'As children in the 1940s waiting for the 81 bus at the top of New

Road, Harlington on the Bath Road, we were always pleased to see the Ashby's Farm lorry returning to Harmondsworth from Brentford Market as this meant a lift home. It was great fun sitting on the empty cabbage boxes.'

❖ THE WAR AND AFTER ❖

'Dad had two allotments, one down the end of Dormers Wells Lane, Southall and one in Lady Margaret Road (nearly down to the Seagull), both quite a distance from Hambrough Road, our home. My sister and I used to help bring home the potatoes in hessian sacks, loaded onto a large old fashioned pushchair (somewhere between today's modern baby chairs and an invalid chair in size). We pushed this old contraption along the pavements, "g-ding, g-ding" over the pavement cracks going up to the allotment (empty barrow) and "g-dong, g-dong" coming home loaded. There were numerous kerbs to negotiate on the way and I remember frantically picking up potatoes scattered everywhere when a sack happened to fall off at a kerb when it wasn't balanced properly. Mum and Dad never got to know what had happened to the precious cargo on the way home on these occasions. At least I don't think they did.

The Lady Margaret Road allotments were between the back of the houses in Lady Margaret Road and the Grand Union Canal. When on the potato run we often took sandwiches, tea for Dad in a Thermos flask, and a bottle of made up drink (cordial). Between the cultivated plots and the canal was a strip of scrubland with a hollow surrounded by hawthorns. We would sit in this hollow and have our picnic, it was also used as a shelter when it rained. Simple paste sandwiches never tasted so good as when we picnicked on the old allotment.

During the war the cry would go up, "Mum, Mum, there's oranges round the corner", and "round the corner" was the greengrocer's in The Broadway, Southall. Frantic grabbing of the shopping bag and money to be dug out of the well-worn black purse, rushing round the corner and standing in the queue (by this time well outside the shop). Watching people coming out with bulging brown paper bags twisted up at the corners, getting into the shop itself, near to the front of the queue and then the notice goes up "Sorry sold out". This didn't always happen of course, sometimes we were lucky and in time to buy.

I remember also going "round the corner" to the Carlton Tuck Shop for my weekly sweet ration, opening the door with the jangling bell, looking up over the high counter and gazing at the assortment of glass jars, with thick stoppers, lined up on the shelves. After a lot of thinking I nearly always finished up with a Mars bar for 6d.

After the end of the war, at the age of eleven, I joined the South Scout Group which was attached to the Congregational church on the corner of Villiers Road and Park Avenue. The Scouts' meeting hall was in Park Avenue over the other side of the road.

We often camped at Chalfont Heights and we transported all our equipment from headquarters in Southall by trek cart. We assembled the trek cart outside the Scout hut, piling on our individual rucksacks, the tents, latrine and cooking screens (hessian poles), billy cans (for cooking on the open fire) etc. We would then take up our positions round the trek cart, in full uniform (wide brim hats and all), two on the handle and two on the guy ropes attached to the wheel axles and the rest behind. Skipper would be solo on his orange tandem bicycle. Off we would go walking all the way to Chalfont Heights, yes, that's right – the other side of Denham in Bucks, mostly along the main Uxbridge Road. The two Scouts on the wooden guiding and pulling handle had to be very careful to keep the cart balanced properly on its one axle, otherwise they could be in for an unexpected ride up in the air, and the whole procession would grind to a halt. It then took the troop "heavies" to bring the cart level and underway again.'

SCHOOLDAYS –
THE BEST YEARS OF OUR LIVES?

*W*et clothes drying round the classroom fire, visits from the
"Nit Nurse", celebrating Empire Day, playground games –
generations of Middlesex children experienced much the same in
their schooldays, but many of us have cause to thank those
hardworking teachers who coped with large classes and little
equipment.

❖ AT BOARDING SCHOOL IN THE 1920s ❖

'I was at boarding school from 1923 to 1931 – eight blissful years.
North Finchley was known as "the village", and Woodside Park
Road ran down to the station where steam trains connected
Finsbury Park to Barnet, and the traffic was mainly horse and
cart.

Two semi-detached Victorian houses had been joined to make
the main building. Four floors were divided between curtained
cubicle dormitories at the top, to the playroom and dark, smelly
cloakroom in the basement, where we spent hours of penance
searching for the lost gym-shoe. Our heavy wooden box desks
were regularly inspected for "tidiness marks" (inkwells to be
kept clean with scraps of pink blotting-paper) and cleaned with
half a lemon then polished on the last day of term. Our piles of
clean laundry were laid out on Saturday morning for the
mending session. Where better to learn running, hemming,
patching and the interminable darning of black woollen
stockings?

Everyone worked for the Junior and Senior Cambridge School
Certificate examinations, finishing with "Matric" in the top form.
Everywhere we went outside the school gates we went in
crocodile – even to cross the road to the school hall or over the
railway bridge to the games field. On Sunday we must have been

115

quite eye-catching on our way to church in white coats, black hats and black stockings! I enjoyed netball, hockey and lacrosse; but the greatest excitement was the weekly visit to the Finchley Road swimming baths in the summer term. An open-top bus took us the three mile journey with juniors inside and seniors upstairs. There was much hilarity if rain made us pull up the canvas covers fixed to the back of the seat in front.

I never remember seeing a newspaper, and, of course, we had

Joining the Scouts and Guides broadened many children's horizons in the 1920s.

no wireless or television. (It was whispered as something shocking that one girl's father was a "Liberal".) But it was a well-regulated, kindly, enclosed existence. Looking back, I think it may have been five years in our Guide company that had the most influence on my adult life. Spit and polish, leadership, patriotism, camping skills – just think what having been leader of the Skylark Patrol would mean in the years to come!'

▣ SCHOOLDAYS AT HAYES IN THE 1930S ▣
'My family moved from South Wales to Hayes in May 1936 and my father, who already worked at Hayes railway station, had enrolled my youngest brother and me into Townfield School, myself in the infants and my brother the senior boys. From the infants' school I eventually progressed up into what was known as the "Hut". This was a wooden structure of about six to eight

Townfield School pupils, Hayes, in 1943.

class-rooms connected by an open veranda. Each room had an iron coal stove, complete with chimney going through the roof. In the winter months the children whose parents could afford to let them buy a bottle of milk used to stand their bottles in the stove's cement surround so that they would be warm when it came to the morning break.

From the Hut I then progressed on to the junior school and I remember the headmaster, Mr Harper, to this day, he always seemed to know your name. I was in Mrs Harris's class and if you did really well at your lessons you were allowed to help in the tuck shop at the morning and afternoon breaks. This was a real honour. She was a very kindly lady with grey hair and I have very fond memories of her as I am sure her other pupils do.

Moving into the senior girls' school was rather traumatic because this was known as "The Big School". You were twelve years old, almost grown up and life began to get very serious. Here you learnt domestic science, cooking and a foreign language.'

▣ EMPIRE DAY IN THE 1930S ▣

'Empire Day, as it was called before the last war, was originally instituted to celebrate Queen Victoria's birthday on 24th May. As a schoolchild in the 1930s it meant only one thing – a half day's holiday. In the morning, dressed in the uniform of whatever organisation we belonged to – Cubs, Brownies, Boys' Brigade etc – we would attend school and after morning prayers we assembled in the playground where we would be addressed by the staff and others of the "great and good" extolling the virtues of our King and Empire. At first we would listen with rapt attention but as children have a very low threshold of boredom when being lectured to by adults, we would soon begin to fidget and whisper amongst ourselves. Once this started our wise headmistress, realizing that our attention was beginning to stray, would immediately order the speeches to end – and announce "playtime".

During this period of play the boys would indulge in a

playground mass mayhem called "British Bulldog". One boy would be selected to stand in the centre of the playground whilst the remainder lined up on one side before charging across to the other without being caught by him. Anyone caught had to join up with the first boy and both would attempt to catch somebody else during the next charge. The charges continued until every charger had been captured at which point the game ended.

Once playtime was over we lined up in our classes and were formally dismissed for the rest of the day. We were all highly delighted at having a half-day holiday, a delight that was slightly tinted with envy as it was rumoured that out in Harefield they had a further half day, not granted to the rest of the county's schoolchildren. Out there, it was said, they had one on 25th April to commemorate Anzac Day but nobody could verify this at the time and, as summer was fast approaching, we soon forgot the matter and got on with the important things in life – cigarette card collecting, marbles and staying out until it was too dark to play anything.'

Pupils of St Andrew's School, Uxbridge in 1940.

'I doubt if any child now has any idea that a yearly day to commemorate our Empire ever existed! We youngsters in the 1930s were very aware of it, especially the pupils at St Nicholas' church school, Shepperton, who were given the afternoon off to celebrate.

That was the nice part, but we really earned that free time as for hours before, our extremely strict teacher drilled us into learning to "salute the flag" in absolute precision.

The whole school had to march (and I *mean* march) into the playground, assemble in complete silence, turn towards the raised Union flag, when – in true sergeant major style – Mr Wakeford would yell, "Salute...the...FLAG!" Up would go our right hand, then smartly down to our side again.

I'm sure it looked very impressive to our parents and the Shepperton VIPs invited to watch, but I remember, above all, how scared I felt in case I made a mistake at the crucial moment and let the school down!'

❖ THE NIT NURSE ❖

'One of the many duties of Nurse Brown was to visit Kingston Road school, Staines several times a year to inspect the children's heads for lice.

I remember her as a quiet kindly sort, plump and dark haired. She wore a brown frock with white starched collar and cuffs and a white starched apron, with a top coat and hat in brown velour.

On the day she came to school, we all had to assemble in the cloakroom. In this large hall with quarry tiled floor, rows of metal pegs and a line of tiny hand-basins along one wall, we had to line up quietly, no conversation was allowed, and one by one she would scrutinize our heads.

I had no idea what a lice was, this was my first inspection and I imagined they must be something like cockroaches or earwigs since they were causing so much fuss – surely one would know if one had them? That day, I didn't. A few days later my brother arrived home from his school with a note for my mother – he had lice!

Mother was fanatical about cleanliness; though there could not have been much money we were always well dressed, she sewed and knitted a lot of our clothes, and kept us spotlessly clean. The note made her very angry indeed. It was an insult to suggest that one of her children had lice and my brother was questioned as to where he had been and who he had sat next to in class.

I was sent to Auntie's shop for paraffin and a stiff brush, and when I got back home my brother's head had been cropped all over. He then had to suffer the paraffin and brush treatment, which my sister and I found highly amusing. We felt no pity for him, obviously influenced by my mother's fury, we thought he was awful to have got lice and would not get near or speak to him for days.

He was not allowed back to school until all signs of this shameful incident had disappeared. Nowadays, we are told that lice are only found in clean heads!'

▣ Disrupted by War ▣

'Our education at Willesden was disrupted by the outbreak of war in 1939. The local schools were evacuated to safer areas and for several months those of us who stayed at home did not attend school. When they reopened lessons were abandoned during air raids and we all took cover in the shelters built in the school grounds. Card games were our usual occupation, the favourite being pontoon, though not for money. The teachers

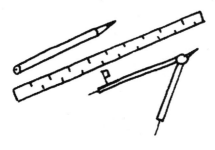

changed frequently, some were called up and some shunted back and forth between the local school site and the town where the school was evacuated to. One night a small bomb hit our school in Willesden and the next day we were taken on a guided tour by the staff to see the demolished classroom.'

◈ WOODTHORPE ROAD SCHOOL, ASHFORD IN 1945 ◈

'In June 1945 I returned from evacuation to live in Ashford. My mother arranged for me to attend Woodthorpe Road school. It was then a senior elementary school for girls. I was twelve years old. The building was large and rather forbidding. The lofty hall was surrounded by classrooms partitioned by wood and glass panels. At the far end was a stage with yet another classroom behind it. To the left of the stage was the headmistress's office and my mother was told to leave me outside the door, she did so and then left. I stood and waited until a short, stout lady appeared and said to me, "Are you the new girl?" "Yes, Miss." "What a rude girl you are, we call the teachers Madam here." "Yes, Madam."

I was allocated to Class 5a where Miss Robinson, a Canadian, was my teacher. She was sympathetic to my situation and encouraged me in every way. I soon realised that I was educationally well ahead of my peers because they had had to spend long hours in shelters during the war whilst my own education had proceeded unhindered, but here the curriculum was fuller with science, geography and the detestable history. Sport played a large part in school life with teams for netball, shinty, rounders, athletics and swimming lessons in the local outdoor pool.

Good discipline was paramount. Teachers were called Madam, pupils opened doors for teachers coming and going and also stood up when an adult entered the room. We did not speak in class unless we were asked to. Lateness or poor work resulted in being sent to Miss Wills, the headmistress, but on the other side of the coin, good work also had to be taken to show her.

We wore ordinary clothes, jumpers (usually hand-knitted) and

122

skirts in winter, and summer dresses in warmer weather. None of us had many clothes because they were still on coupons. We wore either white ankle socks (mine were hand-knitted) or black lisle stockings. No fancy shoes for us, either ankle straps or laced fronts were the order of the day and we had to turn up for school with them polished.

We used pens and ink. We carried satchels over our shoulders. Most of us had our hair either in plaits or bunches tied with satin ribbon. Many of us went home to lunch. We had milk mid-morning.

In the playground we played skipping (including bumps), hopscotch and with balls against the walls. The only toilets the school had were out in the playground and if it rained you got wet! There was no sex education but some girls had booklets about the "birds and bees" and these were passed around surreptitiously and sniggered at.

The teachers were strict but we received a very good education. Some of the foremost teachers in my two happy years were Mrs Catcheside, Miss Vates and Miss Rae. Nobody who was a pupil at Woodthorpe Road school could ever forget Miss Munro, the cookery teacher. Few escaped her command to walk down the stone stairway and across the playground, carrying a glass of hot milk topped with grated nutmeg for Miss Wills' elevenses, with the most terrible threat hanging over their head if they did by any chance spill one drop of milk in the saucer. I soon discovered that you carried the glass in one hand and the saucer in the other.'

▣ PLAYGROUND GAMES ▣

'I spent my primary and junior schooldays at Vaughan schools, West Harrow, and have many happy memories of them. Rather than in the classroom, my own special forte, I now feel, was definitely in the playground. If only there had been a category in the eleven-plus for playground games I would certainly have passed.

There was "swinging on the bars", both the official climbing

123

frame and metal bars protecting the canteen – so many ways of swinging over and under; there was bouncing two and three balls up against the school walls – under the leg and overarm; there was marbles (kept in the felt drawstring bag made by my mother) – aimed through a piece of wood with different sized holes (made by my father), a small one for a "oner" up to a large one for a "fiver"; skipping, both individually (remember the "bumps"?) or the "all together" with an enormously long rope with all the girls in the playground taking turns or going in together; there was "making camps" in the rough ground under the trees – "homes", "dens", etc.

There was hand stands up against a wall with another girl hand-standing in front of your open legs and sometimes even two girls making a stack of three; there was sliding in the snow and ice in the winter and the rather risky game where two children linked arms facing opposite directions, they began to rotate and each was joined by another child, then another and so

on until the whole school was in this two-armed rotating wheel (very fast and I am sure potentially dangerous but I do not remember any fatalities). What happy memories these are, we were so lucky to be allowed such freedom in the playground. I know it is not so now.'

◈ A School in Shepperton in the 1950s ◈

'I came to live in Shepperton in 1952. I had one daughter of six and one son of 18 months. Another daughter was born in 1954. I used to walk up Laleham Road to the farm where there was a working horse, used for pulling the plough, etc. If we were indoors and we heard "clip, clop, clip, clop" we knew that the horse was being led down the road and we followed and watched it being shod at the blacksmith's which was behind the Three Horse Shoes pub.

In 1953 we celebrated Queen Elizabeth's coronation with a party at our house, and they had parties at the schools.

During the war I had lived at Hampton and in the same road

The May Queen procession at Wyatt Road School, Staines in 1959.

there was a teacher from St Nicholas' school who introduced me to the headmaster. I came over to Shepperton to visit the school and remember it was a long low building in the middle of the fields. There were only the houses at the High Street end of Manor Farm Avenue and none of the bungalows.

All children attended assembly with prayers in the main building and then they walked two-by-two crocodile fashion to the various classes in the village. These were held in the Russell Hall, the village hall, the Rifle Range and Thurlestone House. In 1958, new buildings were opened in Manor Farm Avenue. In 1965 eight classrooms in the Hallam Block were built and this saw the end of the classrooms round the village.

Lessons were done with pupils at desks facing the blackboard. The teachers were strict but fair and, although there was a cane, I do not think it was ever used. The deputy head administered "the slipper".

School uniform was compulsory, including hats and caps. Boys were always losing their caps, to be found by big sisters. Plimsolls were worn for sport. Sport consisted of football, rounders and netball. Games played in the playground were hopscotch, skipping (with rhymes), marbles, conkers and whipping tops.

The celebrations which took place were May Day dancing round the maypole, Christmas Nativity plays, school sports and an outing to a farm for the older children. At Christmas children took toys to be given to Barnardo's. Children learnt to cook by watching their mothers. I do not know what craft the boys did but the girls learnt cross-stitch and knitted clothes with thick wool and big needles.'

THE WORLD OF WORK

ON THE LAND

Farming was a way of life for many people in the county, some villages being completely rural in character. Life on the land has changed so much in the last 50 years, since the days when the horse provided the power and farm work was labour intensive and a part of the seasonal calendar.

▣ BORN ON A RUISLIP FARM ▣

'In 1924, when I was born, we lived on a farm in Ruislip. When I was about four years old my mother took me shopping by pony and trap to Ruislip village shops. The horse trough was then in the middle of the road at the junction of High Street and Bury Street. She left me in the trap whilst shopping in Haileys the post office which backed onto the duck pond. I was standing up and when the pony moved to drink from the trough I fell out of the trap onto the pavement outside Mrs Bray's sweet shop!

My father used to take a horse and cart with a load of hay, chaff, or pea and bean sticks to Hammersmith or the Isleworth area. He would leave early in the morning and return after dark. He was courting my mother, then living at Priors Farm by the Western Avenue. He stopped there and sent the horse and cart home towards Harefield; after walking home across the fields the horse would be waiting for him in the yard.

Other times, when tired, the men could get into the bottom of the van (a cart has two, a van has four wheels) cover themselves with sacks to sleep, and their horse would bring the van home, for the men to be woken up by the dog greeting them in the yard. The pea and bean sticks were coppiced from Bayhurst, Copse and Park Woods for delivery to the London merchants.

In the late 1920s a fair was held in Ruislip High Street once a year, similar to that still held in Pinner. There used to be dancing round the horse trough on New Year's Eve when the old George

Jim Collins and his cart at Ruislip in the 1920s.

pub turned out. The trough has since been resited near the war memorial.

On "pea-soup" foggy nights, the Ruislip-Northwood Council used to put out flares in Ruislip High Street. The flares were like an overgrown watering can with a flare out of the spout and were used to indicate road junctions.

In the middle 1930s, after school, my mother would send me down to the fields with my Dad's tea, then I had to work pulling the drag rake behind me up and down the field until dark. The drag rake had steel "claws" and was about four feet wide.

If still light and the hay was ready we would bring it home to build up the hay ricks. Bands or ropes of hay were made by hand to tie up the trusses of hay.

There wasn't much time for play after school for farm children. The chaff cutter was in use most evenings, particularly if there was an order for chaff to feed horses. Chaff is hay cut into half-inch lengths on a machine consisting of a wheel about four to five feet in diameter with two very sharp knives built into it. The wheel was turned by hand like a big mincing machine; no guards on the knives or the cogs where the hay was fed in, and very hard work if the knives were blunt.

I started work at Christmas after my 14th birthday at Gurney & Ewers, now EMI in Bury Street, Ruislip. At 6 am on my own, I would creep in through the sliding door, the rats would run away when I switched on the light, then I had to put a firework into the Blackstone generator. When the firework went off I put a one inch steel bar about three feet long into a hole in the big fly wheel to make the wheel rotate, but making sure I dragged the bar out before it hit the floor and hurt me! All this on my own – 14 years old – about 1939. Then I had to light the fire in the boiler house in the old ship boiler to raise a head of steam to turn the machinery. Often the police would come in for a cup of tea about 7.30 am before going off shift at 8 am.'

◈ A COMPLETELY RURAL VILLAGE ◈

'In the 1920s Ickenham was a completely rural village with a two-class society. The gentry lived in the large houses, Swakeleys being the most notable, with the villagers working either in the house or as farmworkers, gardeners, grooms, etc. The staff were generally very happy and well treated but were always expected to nod or raise a cap when passing the owners of the big house. At Swakeleys there was a beautiful lake which during icy winters would be used for skating, one end for the gentry and the other for the villagers.

Ickenham was well known for its hay production in earlier generations. Farmers would take bales of hay, hand cut with a huge hay-knife and tied with bands, up to London by horse and waggon leaving the village at 3 am and return with a load of manure from the City stables.

I came to Ickenham in 1941 to work as a land girl on a retail dairy farm owned by a member of an old Ickenham family, situated in the centre of the village. The cows were all milked by hand and the milk strained, cooled (no sterilising in those days), bottled and delivered by pony and cart, either the same or

The Manor Farm at Ickenham in about 1910.

following day. Our work started at 6 am and during haymaking and harvest went on until late evening.

At harvest time the corn was put in "stooks" and after about three weeks, having been stacked in the field to dry, was brought up to the farmyard and built into ricks which were then expertly thatched to await the thresher later in the year. Swedes, kale and mangolds were grown for the cows and had to be hoed and cut at the appropriate time.'

❖ Mint a Speciality ❖
'Each late spring and early summer in the 1930s, my friend Olive and her husband would be woken, in the early hours, by women and girls singing and laughing as they walked the two or three miles from their homes in Ashford, along the winding road, to Mr Barker's farm in Laleham. They were the mint pickers. Their working hours started at 4 am and finished at 4 pm.

Mr Barker farmed 280 acres which he rented from the Lucan

Estates. When Olive started work in his office, she was instructed that the letters she typed to be sent to the then Lord Lucan were not finished with a "Yours faithfully". The correct valediction was "Believe me, my dear Lord".

Large shire horses tilled the land. Mr Barker's crops included all vegetables which were commercially saleable. He did not go in for fruit except for raspberries. These were big and succulent, being one of his specialities. Another speciality was mint.

When ready, the mint would be gathered from the fields and put on long trestle tables in front of the barn. Here it would be picked over and the weeds, which had grown with it, extracted by hand. As the weeds included stinging nettles and thistles this was not a painless task. However, the pickers, being on piece-work rates, got on with the job. The picked-over mint was packed into trays which were loaded onto lorries. At 4 am the next day the lorries were driven up to Covent Garden. The major purchaser of the mint was the manufacturer of "Mellor's Mint Sauce".

Mr Barker's farm is no more. Some of the land is still used for agricultural purposes. The rest has been given over to housing and to gravel raising.'

OTHER WAYS WE EARNED A LIVING

There were so many other ways we earned a living that these can be only a small selection of memories – from the village blacksmith to the midwife, the builder to the Royal Photographer.

▣ BLACKSMITH, WHEELWRIGHT AND UNDERTAKER ▣

'My father, uncle, grandfather and great grandfather were the village blacksmiths, wheelwrights and undertakers at Stanwell. My father and uncle carried on the business after their father died in the very early 1920s.

When he was a lad of five, my father's job was to stand on a box and work the hand-operated bellows. After leaving school aged eleven, he worked as a houseboy for three shillings a week. On returning to the forge at the age of 15, he earned six shillings a week and then moved to smithies in Hounslow, Egham, Tooting and Hertfordshire before coming back to Stanwell. There was often enough work to keep them busy from 6 am to 8 pm. Pony shoeing at that time was three shillings for a set of four. Once he was asked to shoe the feet of an eight-legged horse, a circus freak which had short legs growing from each fetlock.

My sister, brother and I often watched the coffins being made, cut and turned into shape from great tree trunks. Babies' coffins were lined with beautiful white embossed material and my mother made little pillows for them. My father was the smith but also helped my uncle with the funerals. The children loved watching Dad shoe the horses. They also repaired the farm carts, mainly broken wheels which often needed new rings (tyres); these were made from iron, heated on a bonfire and then burnt onto the wheels until they fitted tight, iron rivets were then knocked in to hold them fast.

We lived one side of the village green and the village shop was the other side; it was very small, but sold everything from a pin

Cole's smithy at Stanwell, a family business until the 1970s.

to an elephant, as we used to say. Nothing was sold in packets everything had to be weighed and the bill added up. It also housed the post office and there was a bake house at the back where bread was made every morning and delivered to the neighbouring villages, also hot cross buns were delivered *hot* on Good Friday morning, in time for breakfast. In the early 1930s three cottages attached to the shop were demolished and the shop extended, with three flats above. I went to work there in 1938 when I was 18, when almost everything still had to be weighed, which was as well when the war came and food was rationed. We worked from 7.30 am till 8 pm with an hour off for lunch when the shop closed from 1 to 2 pm, half day was Wednesday. We were actually working on the Sunday morning (unpaid overtime) when war was declared; we were at the back of the shop weighing and wrapping some of the dry goods when the siren which was right opposite the shop sounded, so I downed tools and went home.

In 1937 my father and uncle dissolved partnership and we moved a little way up the road. The undertaking business had finished by then but my father had permission from the council to open his forge at the side of the house and carried on his shoeing business until two years before he died in 1973. The family business ended then as my brother was never interested in it.'

◫ The Shop at Twickenham ◫

'My grandparents ran a grocery shop in Church Street, Twickenham, for around 50 years, and for many of the early years my grandmother served out not only groceries but also basic, sensible medical advice!

Around 1901 the young couple travelled down to Twickenham by train, and decided to rent a double-fronted shop in Church Street – later they bought the premises, which had two floors of living accommodation above and a large cellar below. My grandfather came from a family grocery business in Bristol, but had served as an army medical orderly in India and South Africa. He was described on his marriage certificate as a "male nurse". Grandma was also a nurse – trained in London, but nursing at an army hospital in Aldershot when they married. Thus, she was exchanging the starched uniform of a nurse for an equally crisp overall for the shop, so perhaps it was natural for her to still practise her nursing skills! In those days when a visit to the doctor resulted in a bill you hesitated to consult him over childish spots, coughs or tumbles, or over your own ailments. Even if you were a "panel patient" and the cost was not such a worry, how convenient to combine your bit of shopping with asking a trained nurse to "have a look or listen". I gather my grandmother had a good relationship with the local doctor, who guessed she would send him patients as necessary.

Shop hours were long, and even worse on Saturdays when tables would be put out on the pavement for an outdoor market until late in the evening. I gather this did not last for many years

– probably to their great relief. Sundays were the only leisure day, apart from early closing on Wednesdays, and on Sunday my grandparents, and later their two children took walks along the riverside, and later bicycle trips to places such as Sunbury and Shepperton. Rural Middlesex was probably rather attractive to cyclists – nice and flat, and full of market gardens. I believe many of the nursery gardens did a side-line in selling teas and lemonade – very welcome!

Work in the shop was also arduous, and many provisions were delivered in bulk, and had to be weighed out and packaged. Stiff blue paper was shaped into "pokes", or little bags, for sugar, dried fruit and tapioca etc. These bags were then stored in large wooden-topped metal bins, which lined one side of the shop. Above them were smaller bins for spices, ginger and such like. Above these were huge black and gold decorated bins for teas and coffee, but many of these large bins were simply for decoration, as they were too heavy to lift if full! Biscuits were sold from glass-topped metal boxes. I remember these so well as a child, and fear they set me off on a lifetime addiction to eating too many biscuits – it was always a challenge to try one from each tin!

One side of the shop was devoted to dairy produce, and had a marble counter instead of polished wood. A large bacon slicing

machine dispensed bacon cut to the customer's requirements for thickness – the shop assistant was expected to remember! A cheese board, complete with cheese-cutting wire was always "out of bounds" to me as a child. Eggs were sold loose and put into bags with a bed of straw from the crate they arrived in from the Suffolk farm which sent eggs direct to Twickenham station every week or so. My grandparents occasionally sent their children down to the farm for holidays, but they had to keep the shop open all the year around.

Hardware was sold in the shop for many years, as well as paraffin oil and vinegar from barrels kept in the cellar. Customers would bring in bottles to be filled. I have wondered since how everything was fitted into a relatively small shop, but I suppose there was not the huge variety of every commodity then. Soup was either tinned tomato or oxtail, cheese was Cheddar and washing products were bar soap and a blue bag!

Regular shoppers were able to have their orders delivered by a boy on a vast bicycle fitted with a metal container for the boxes. I get the impression that the boy was not a full-time employee, but probably worked after school. Some items in the shop were kept specifically for orders, there not being a great demand for them. Regulars also got a Christmas gift from the shopkeeper – a calendar, or a small box of biscuits or dried fruit. These would be decided upon months before, and ordered from the travellers who called in regularly. They were always seen in the tiny office at the back of the shop and entertained to tea if they were in favour at the time!

One disadvantage of living over the shop was that you were apt to be aroused by frenzied ringing on the bell by a customer who had just gone to the tea caddy and found it empty! My grandmother was also liable to be called upon to do a neat bandaging job if some child had gashed its knee. After some 20 years or so my grandparents moved to live elsewhere in Twickenham, and only used the rooms above for storage – they were also glad to get a small garden then. They never kept a shop cat, as there wasn't a garden, and relied on the famous "Little

Nipper" mousetraps, which they also sold. I expect mice were a problem with cereals delivered in sacks.

My grandparents ran the shop until around 1952 when they retired. The family who took over kept it as a grocery and until 1960 when I got married, and for a good many years after, it was still possible to leave my order one day and receive it the next. By then it was delivered by van. Very soon, of course, supermarkets arrived everywhere, and our shopping habits changed for ever.'

◙ THE PEARCY BROTHERS ◙

'The Pearcy brothers, Tom and Jack, sons of a butcher, left the British army after the First World War with no job to go to and could not afford their own shop. So they purchased a secondhand sausage machine and proceeded to manufacture pounds and pounds of pork sausages on the kitchen table of their mother's house in St Margaret's Grove, St Margaret's, Twickenham. Having acquired a horse and cart, they went around the streets locally selling them from house to house, and they soon became well known and the venture a great success. Eventually they were able to afford to open their own butcher's shop at 44 Winchester Road, St Margaret's in the mid-1920s. Jack died in the early 1930s but Tom carried on till 1950 when he retired to the south coast.'

◙ A LONDON FASHION HOUSE ◙

'In 1947 I started work in a London fashion house, sewing luxury items for ladies and children. In the war years there had been certain restrictions on the amount of fine stitching allowed on any one garment, eg "Fine stitching not to exceed twice the bust measurement of the customer". This ruling had been relaxed by the time I started work.

Through that notoriously bitter winter of 1947 the heating was almost nil, and there was no running hot water. As our fingers became too stiff to work properly, we filled bowls with nearly boiling water from a kettle and "bathed" our hands until a spark

Tom Pearcy outside his butcher's shop at St Margarets, Twickenham in 1930.

of life returned, enabling us to continue work. As ours were sedentary jobs we felt the extreme cold throughout our bodies, particularly around the feet. Eventually someone had the brainwave of finding cardboard boxes to put our feet in, which improved things immensely. It seems strange to recall those early primitive conditions, which thankfully improved vastly over the years.'

▣ FAIREY AVIATION ▣
'Before and during the Second World War the Fairey Aviation Company, which at the time was a family concern, owned an aerodrome close to Heathrow, a small village on the Bath Road, where they tested their new aircraft, one of which was the world famous Fairey Firefly. It was nothing out of the ordinary to see parts of aircraft wings, bodies or complete engines, being

transported around the district on large lorries for assembly at the airfield. Unfortunately their Senior Test Pilot, Fl Lt Chris Stanland, was killed in a flying accident at the aerodrome during the war. The owner's son, Dick Fairey, was involved in a serious flying accident whilst serving with the Air Force during the war; he was shot down and "ditched" in the Channel, losing both his legs. After the war he flew a helicopter which almost daily landed in a field beside the factory at Hayes and was a familiar sight to be seen. Another pre-war test pilot was Fred Dixon. My brother, Jack, who was an apprentice with the firm in 1938/40 was fortunate to take a few routine trips with both these test pilots, and after flying with the RAF during the war made his career as a civilian pilot.

At the end of the war the Government compulsorily purchased the Heathrow aerodrome from the Fairey Aviation Company for one million pounds and included the old civil aerodrome at Heston in the deal. Fairey's Heathrow aerodrome was the start of the now famous International London (Heathrow) Airport.

Unfortunately, the Heston aerodrome proved too small for the new larger aircraft being built by Fairey and so it had to be closed. Also the Fairey factory at Hayes stopped producing aircraft, as we knew them, and went into the production of helicopters, and was eventually taken over by another helicopter firm which moved away from Hayes altogether.

To commemorate the Heston aerodrome's existence a brand new council estate was built on the land and was called the "Aerodrome Estate". To this day when you enter or leave the estate there is a large iron sign saying "Aerodrome" and showing a model of one of Fairey's original aircraft.'

▣ THE FACTORY HOOTERS ▣

'One of my most vivid memories as a child before the Second World War was the early morning factory hooters. In the area surrounding Hayes station there were at least four large factories – His Master's Voice Gramophone Company, Nestlé's chocolate factory, Fairey Aviation Company and Kraft Cheese, besides

140

smaller ones like the X-Chair furniture factory and Scotts jam factory. Each one of these factories had their own hooter with its own pitch to remind their workers that if they didn't hurry they would be late for work. Also in the distance you could hear the Southall hooters sounding off. I would lie in bed between 6.30 and 7.30 am and identify each hooter as it sounded. Then in the evening the hooters would sound again to say that the working day was over. I can remember my mother saying to me when the Fairey Aviation one sounded, "Lay the table girl, the boys will be home in 15 minutes, hungry for their dinner and we mustn't keep them waiting."

In those days cars were a luxury and public transport was very scarce, so the workers had to either cycle to and from work or walk. I remember seeing Coldharbour Lane five deep with cyclists, and just as many walking along the pavements, mostly men and happily chatting away to their work colleagues as they went. The sound of human voices was a joy to hear.'

▣ BOOTS THE CHEMIST ▣

'Before my children came along I worked for Boots the Chemist, Hounslow. I was head of the Fancy Goods Department. This meant ordering and selling handbags, jewellery, leather goods, glass and china, kitchen ware, vacuum flasks and accessories, greeting cards and many miscellaneous items. We served the customers in those days and when helping them with their purchases we always remembered to be polite, interested and helpful. The customer was *always* right and the aim was to send them away happy and satisfied for them to return at a later date. We did have a large electric till (very modern then) but purchases had to be wrapped in brown paper from a big roll slung underneath the till. Only small items such as brooches or necklaces were put into boxes or small bags.

I worked a six day week nine o'clock to six o'clock with half day closing on a Wednesday afternoon and was paid just over £5 every fortnight. Funnily, it did not seem like hard work at the time though how I worked all day on three inch stiletto heels I will never know.'

141

◙ Working in a Bank ◙

'Jobs were a lot easier to find in the 1950s although I had not found it easy to get into the bank, and only found an opening for a girl because the lads were being called up to do their National Service and in those days lady staff were kept on as temporary staff before becoming permanent. The bank seemed to me even then to be living in another age. I had never before been addressed so formally and had never ever been greeted by a gentleman carrying a neatly rolled umbrella and wearing a trilby hat, which was raised every time he said "Good morning". I was so nervous on my first day that I slipped and fell down the wooden stairs which led to the safes below. Things did relax a little later in the day, after the doors were closed to the public at 3 pm. The gentlemen were allowed to take off their suit jackets; suits had to be worn every day by the men excepting Saturday morning when sports jackets were allowed. Then came the task of balancing the books at the end of the day; cashiers were responsible for balancing their own tills, and everything had to be listed and agreed before sending cheques off to Head Office at the end of each day. We did not leave before all was correct which meant working late on quite a few occasions. There was no overtime payment, but we did qualify for 3s 6d tea money if we worked after 6.30 pm.'

◙ At the Met Office ◙

'In September 1947, I left school at the age of 17 from Blaina, Gwent (then Monmouthshire), a small town in South Wales. In those days, the only option for girls was nursing or teaching. Neither attracted me, and then I saw an advertisement for a career in the Meteorological Office on our school notice board. This appealed to me as meteorology was included in our geography lessons in my last year. I applied, was accepted, and began my training at the Air Ministry in Holborn. Yes, there really was an Air Ministry roof!

After six weeks' training, I hoped to return to a post in South Wales, but this was not to be and I found I had been posted to one of the then headquarters at Harrow. I spent twelve very happy years there until the office moved to the now main headquarters at Bracknell. Having married in the meantime, I was unable to continue my career at Bracknell.

I met many interesting people during my time at Harrow, not least the Father of Radar, Sir Robert Watson-Watt, who attended an Open Day at the office at which I was his guide around the building. Several television personalities worked with me in Harrow such as John Parry (the original presenter) and later Graham Parker and Barbara Edwards, the first female presenter.'

◙ THE ROYAL PHOTOGRAPHER ◙

'My thoughts often go back to the ten happy years, 1946 to 1956, I spent working for Mr Baron, the Royal Photographer. The studios were situated in Brick Street just off Park Lane. The "Steering Wheel Club" was below, to which Stirling Moss was a frequent visitor.

One of my first duties was to deliver an item to Buckingham Palace. Although sitting in an old taxi I felt quite important as we drove through the gates. I was tempted to give that special wave to the many tourists standing around!

As time passed the business expanded from ten members of staff to over 30, busy with fashion photography and even cookery items which were published in a women's magazine, also many photocalls, including ballet.

Being the production assistant it was my job to make sure orders were passed to each department, with an irate call from Baron if a certain order was not ready. We had many celebrities being photographed. Fortunately with my job I was able to find out, by looking through a large crack in the studio door, who was actually being photographed. On one occasion it was Danny Kaye, so I and two other girls crept along to have a peep. On hearing Baron's footsteps coming towards the door we panicked and my arm was caught in the other girl's necklace. The sound of those unknotted pearls falling on the parquet flooring was an absolute nightmare!

143

In 1951 we had a new member of staff join us by the name of Tony Armstrong-Jones. I was photographed with him solely for the benefit of testing a new camera. This photo was published at a later date to announce his engagement to Princess Margaret.

So many exciting times to recall whilst working here, but nothing to match a certain day in March 1953. Baron rushed into our office and yelled "Maggles (that was my nickname), I need you for Buckingham Palace." Apparently I had to stand in for the Queen in preparation for the Coronation photos. Our sales director joined me as the Duke of Edinburgh. After the photo session the Queen appeared and I duly curtsied and shook hands with her. The Duke of Edinburgh came over and shook hands with us all. Prince Charles, in the meantime, was most interested in the photographic equipment.'

❖ A Small Builder ❖

'In the 1950s there were still many rented properties managed for their owners by estate agents and as a small builder I carried out various repairs to quite a few in the area around Hounslow. Jobs as varied as replacing slipped or broken slates, renewing hot and cold water tanks and repairing burst lead pipes, hanging new doors and gates etc, in fact attending to every defect with the sole exception of electrical problems.

Naturally as each job usually differed from the last a large number of tools were required to cope and these, plus ladders and if it was a two handed task, an assistant, were all transported by successively a Fordson van, an Austin pick-up truck and finally a Morris mini-bus.

Materials were readily obtained from one of the local builders merchants, usually Sparrows or the Standard Wallpaper Company which despite its name carried in stock practically everything to do with the building trade and the staff in both shops were helpful and cheery as well as being most knowledgeable. In the winter the Standard, as it was known, was heated by a large cast iron barrel stove which was dismantled and removed from the shop each springtime. The erecting and the first lighting of this stove at the onset of the cold weather was a well known ceremony amongst the trade and usually up to half a dozen builders would gather in the shop on the appointed day to witness this "Official Start" to the winter.

During this period I got to know many of the tenants of the houses quite well. One old lady who in her late seventies was still working in the fields around Bedfont, wore a man's cap and a sacking apron, called her 50 year old son "Young Charlie" and referred to her glasses as "bicycle focals", and the eccentric headmistress who picked winners by the simple expedient of backing every horse in the race, are but two of the many who invited me in for a "cuppa" during those years.

The numerous working men's cafes played an important role in my life in those days, serving as temporary offices where some advanced planning for the next job on the list could be pondered over and thought through and also as a meeting place for seeing colleagues and rivals and indulging in some light-hearted mickey taking with both groups. "Caffs" were plentiful, well populated and the atmosphere, even on a miserably wet or freezing cold day was one of joviality. Such places have now largely disappeared and with their demise the joy of sitting down to a mid-morning bacon and egg "sarni"or if ravenously hungry, the delights of a full fried breakfast and two buttered slices.

Nowadays of course, unless sandwiches are brought from home it's some microwaved product from a local baker's or fast food outlet and very often eaten in a hurry, and with the "frank and open" discussions on every subject under the sun which were such features of our cafe society in the 1950s, alas, along with those cafes, gone for ever!'

MIDWIFE AT SHEPPERTON

'I always wanted to be a nurse and I've got to thank Hitler for one thing. Once the war was on I didn't have to pay for my training. I did this at Ashford Hospital, making out I was 22 instead of 32. Mind you, Matron and the tutors knew. I loved every minute of my training there, where we were looking after Germans and Italians as well as our own boys. I became a Sister.

After the war a gang of us who had worked together decided to do midwifery in London. I trained at the Salvation Army Mothers Hospital and hated it. I was frightened out of my life. I passed the exams, but came back to general nursing. Then in 1951 Miss Greeno said she wanted a midwife in Shepperton. I didn't know what to do. I was cycling home from Ashford Hospital that evening, and I said to myself "If there's a light in Miss Greeno's house when I pass it, I'll call in and say 'yes'. If there's no light, I won't do the job." There was a light, so I went back to midwifery.

There was no refresher course, and I had to learn to drive. The first time I went out with the BSM instructor I knocked a low garden wall down. We went up to the house, found the front door open, and there was this old gentleman in bed. I was still in my uniform and he said, "Thank goodness you've come, my girl, I want the bottle." He thought I was his regular nurse, but I found a bottle and gave it to him. The BSM people went back the next day and rebuilt the wall.

My very first case was a mother living in Laleham Road. When I saw that little head arriving, oh, I'll never forget it. I was terrified and wanted to run home. I never let on it was my first delivery for six years. Everything was all right, but when I got home I was soaked with perspiration.

Another time, when I was substituting for another midwife a man rang up from Green Lane, Sunbury. He told me his wife was in labour and asked if he should ring up the television people. He told me he worked for BBC TV and that the birth was going to be televised. I said "No, it isn't. I'm not having TV people in while I'm delivering." However, I rang the office and they told me to carry on and do it. When I arrived at the house the bedroom was full of wires and lights and there were five or six men. The lights were so hot I could hardly breathe. Then the producer asked, "What happens if one of my men faints?"

I said, "That will be just too bad."

He said, "Well, some of them aren't married, you know."

146

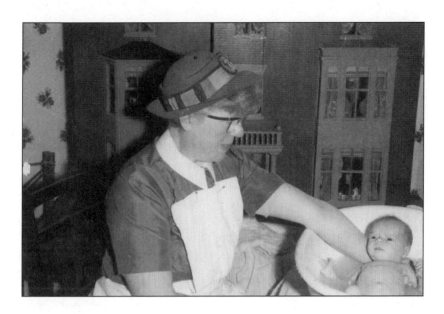

Sister Doris Naylor in 1960, Shepperton's much loved midwife.

"If they faint, they faint," I told him. "It's nothing to do with me."

The mother had the baby all right, and they televised it all, recording its first cry and even the first sucking noise as I put her to the mother's breast. After the filming was over, and the baby had been recorded being bathed and weighed, the men all shook my hand. The ones who weren't married said, "Well, if we have a baby we won't mind having it at home if you come."

This ended up as a film for TV called *The Body*. It was part of a series, and this birth came in the middle. It was educational, to let people know that it was safe for babies to be born at home. It went on Schools programmes for years. I was asked by all the local schools, St Nicholas, Bishop Wand and Thamesmead, to talk it through. Kids used to say, "That's her, that's her!"

I had another case, an Australian couple who had rented a house in Broadlands Avenue, Shepperton. He worked in Fleet Street, and they were very wealthy. It was their third child, but in those days you couldn't have your baby in hospital unless you were over 29, because they were full up. This couple were very apprehensive about having it at home because they'd never heard of it in Australia. Well, the birth was fine and she had a little girl. They were so delighted that afterwards they took me out to the Ritz. I put on my best frock and was treated like a queen.

Other families were very poor, with nowhere to put the new baby. Many's the time I've lined a drawer and put the baby in that. We usually managed to take in things for the baby if we knew they didn't have much, and then the Health Visitor would come along and we'd manage to get a cradle and a pram for it.

I never lost a baby, and I delivered 1,300 of them. We had very good doctors who would come out immediately if I wanted them, and we'd get the mother to hospital right away. I could smell a rat, and knew if anything was wrong. I remember one mother, she was unmarried and it was her first baby. She was a long time in labour, so I rang the doctor and told him, and asked for an ambulance to get her to Ashford Hospital. Well, we were dashing along when the ambulance went over the bridge over Halliford Halt and she had the baby in the ambulance. I knocked on the window and told the driver there was no need to go to the hospital. So we went back to her home. I think the bump over the bridge did it.

Then once I called out the doctor for a forceps delivery. There's a big caravan site, Grange Farm, in Halliford. In those days the caravans were like little boxes, and you had to step on to a wooden box to get into them. The doctor came from Walton and as he stepped on to this wooden box with his black bag his foot went straight through. He got it out and carried on. It was a safe forceps delivery, but he said, "Don't you dare ask me to deliver a baby in a caravan again. I'll never come." He was serious. Mind you, the space was so small and there was no water, we had to get it from the standpipe. It was so primitive.

I've also delivered babies on boats on the river. Doctors aren't very keen, there's usually only a small cabin, but often the mother wants it at home. I've also delivered them on the two islands on the Thames here, Pharoahs and Hamhaugh. Of course

I had to be ferried over. One particular June night I delivered a lovely baby to a woman on Pharoahs Island and left about three o'clock in the morning. The father ferried me back across and I remember it was a full moon. I was looking at my car on the mainland and the moon shone on the water and made it look like grass, so I stepped out of the boat into the river. I was up to my neck, still holding my midder bag. Well I got out dripping and coated with that horrid green stuff. I covered the seat of my car with the mackintosh sheets I used for my mothers, and as I got in the car I could hear that man laughing all the way back to the island!

I belong to the Shepperton Amateur Dramatic Society, and I was all dressed up and on the stage when a chap's head came round the door and he asked for me. I went just as I was. My midder bag was in my car, of course, and I stripped off when I got there. The baby was born OK. Then many times I've gone out in thick snow.

Once I had two women in labour in Watersplash Road at the same time. I was running back and forth in the snow delivering the babies. I got the Boy Scouts to dig my car out.

Down Russell Road in Shepperton there was a Romany caravan site. It was on the left side as you go down towards Marshalls Garage, where the Mulberry Trees estate is now. The Romanies bought that land because they went out in the summer to all the fairs, and they always worked it that they had their babies in the winter there.They arrived in October and left again at Easter. They were very nice, very gentle people and had strong family ties. There was the mother, the grandmother, and the great grandmother, helping each other. The men used to call for me and say, "My wife's in labour." I'd follow them down to Russell Road and attend to the mother and these men would walk round and round the caravan until the baby was born. Then they'd go away and all the women would crowd in.

Their caravans were lovely, very clean and colourful. You could eat off the floor. The children belonging to the camp were clean and spotless, too. They had their babies easily, I think it was because the old grannies used to give the mothers herbs and all sorts of things from the fields. It was their secret and I never asked them. They never went to antenatal clinics, and they never went near a doctor.

Then suddenly all the Romanies left and we got tinkers on the field. They were horrible, coarse and filthy. They had dog fights and cock fights, even while I was there delivering a baby. I got the police in then. They were there on that field until they started building the houses, but it took the police to get them off the site.

I got used to broken nights. Sometimes I'd go to bed at ten, be woken up at eleven, come home at two and go out again and return at five in the morning. Then I'd have my day's work the next day. Even when you were off duty fathers would come for you. When I was out I always left an address chalked on a slate in my window, with a phone number.'

A Large Enfield Nursery

'The nursery managed by my father at turn-of-the-century Enfield consisted of several acres of ground with 30 greenhouses in which were grown many varieties of non-flowering plants, specialising in ferns. The majority were despatched to the docks to decorate the ships of the P&O and Cunard lines. Each plant was wrapped in white paper, packed in large wooden egg boxes obtained from biscuit manufacturers who bought their eggs from Holland. The completed orders were taken to the station by a horse and trolley.

The ferns were increased by the propagation of those little brown spots on the back of the leaves (spores). This was a skilled job which was carried out in special houses at a high temperature. It was interesting and fascinating to watch the development of these tiny spores into beautiful ferns, including asparagus and maidenhair. The houses were heated in the winter by pipes – tons of coke were used to keep the furnaces alight. There were also large tanks of water to keep the summer watering going.

The nursery also included an orchard with apples, pears and Victoria plum trees. How lovely it looked in the spring. There

was a profusion of wild flowers in the hedges and ditches –
marguerites, poppies, sweet scented violets, blue and white
comfrey and, of course, buttercups and daisies. The grass was
allowed to grow to feed the horse – we had our own haymaking
time which was good fun.

The rest of the grounds were cultivated – hundreds of outdoor
tomatoes were grown and ripened, roses, and the now old-
fashioned red clove carnations, beautifully scented. All crops
including hard fruits were sent to Covent Garden market.'

◈ A LONDON LAUNDRY ◈

'When we came to live in Chiswick in the 1960s, I used to take the
household washing to the Pier House Laundry, in Strand-on-the-
Green near Kew Bridge. The laundry was in a rather handsome
long red-brick building facing the river. We thought it was quite
expensive – shirts cost 1s 5d, sheets 1s, and pillowcases 6d. But
that was for the First Class Service – you could save by having a
machine-wash (eg bath towels 6d), or you could bring a whole
bag to be washed in "Q" blue, ready for ironing at home, for 3s.
City gents had their white shirts delivered beautifully wrapped
in blue tissue paper, and a week's supply of starched collars in
special square boxes, six to a box.

The laundry had been opened in 1860 by an emigré French
chef called Camille Simon and his wife, a laundress from Toulon.
Dissatisfied with the quality of English soap powders, they
imported their own from France. This washed whiter than white
and the laundry flourished and became one of the biggest in
London. Naturally, other laundries wanted the soap powder,

Working at the Pier House Laundry, Chiswick, ironing and in the packing room.

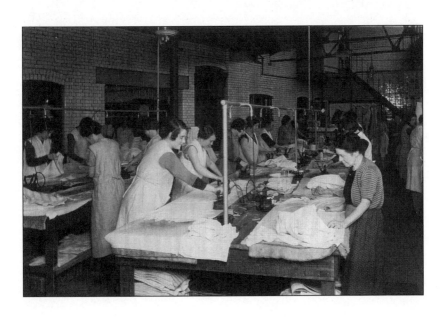

Villages relied on local shops and services, such as the post office and stores at Ickenham in the 1920s.

and in 1898 Simon registered it as "Simon's Lessive Cleansing Extract of Soap" and set up a company to manufacture it. In due course it was not only in use in British hospitals, laundries and workhouses, but exported to most parts of the world. The family (Simon had seven children and his sons followed him into the business) gave up laundering and concentrated on producing the soap powder, both their own "Q" range (called after Kew) which you can still buy, and powders for the big supermarket chains to sell as "own brands" – though some, like Sainsbury's, have since replaced them with powders they produce themselves.

Meanwhile the laundry continued, surviving floods when the Thames burst its banks, and the wartime bombs which fell rather thickly round here as the German bombers used to follow the river and Kew Bridge was one of their targets – they missed the bridge, but destroyed all but the cellar of the old City Barge pub a bit further down the road. Many local people worked in the laundry (though one I know of found it too hot and steamy and had to leave), so it was a blow when it closed in 1973. By then laundrettes had sprung up or people had home washing machines.'

WAR & PEACE

The Great War 1914–1918

The war brought danger to the civilians of Middlesex, as Zeppelins droned overhead, and it also brought the war wounded to the county.

▣ ZEPPELIN! ▣

'I was born in Southall in 1911. My earliest memories are from the First World War when my sister and I were wrapped in blankets and taken to shelter from the Zeppelin bombing. The night they strafed Brentford we were taken into the stables of a builder's yard opposite our home, which was a butcher's business run by my father.'

'Born in Enfield, my earliest recollections are of being put to bed under a much scrubbed kitchen wooden table with Mother urging my older brother and sister to sing a prayer they had learnt at school:

> "Lord keep us safe this night,
> Secure from all our fears,
> May angels guard us while we sleep,
> Till morning light appears."

Then my father snatching me in his arms, carrying me to the front door to see a blazing Zepplin in the sky, shot down by Fl Lt Robinson over nearby Cuffley, where a memorial still stands. Senior lads of the Boys' Brigade rode around on their bicycles sounding the all clear on their bugles when the guns ceased firing.'

◙ WAR WORK ◙

'My mother, who was a young woman at the time of the First World War, was directed into doing "war work". She operated a sewing machine making gas masks for the soldiers who were fighting in the trenches in France.

After completion the gas masks were closely scrutinised for strayed stitches that would leave a highly dangerous gap. Woe betide the seamstress found guilty of this crime, she would be reduced to tears by the foreman's stern warning: "Do you realise that one of our boys could be gassed because of your sloppy work?"

All this history took place in a room beneath the stadium at Tottenham football ground.'

◙ HAREFIELD HOSPITAL ◙

'The hospital was built in the grounds of a stately house (called Harefield Park House) especially for wounded Australian and New Zealand soldiers, and the local villagers used to visit and care for them as they were so far from home.

A First World War postcard, issued after the King and Queen had visited wounded ANZAC soldiers at Harefield Hospital.

The soldiers who died were buried in a very special part of St Mary's churchyard which is kept in order to this day by the War Graves Commissioners. After the war a memorial was erected in the middle of the stones and every year on 25th April, known as Anzac day, the local school-children march from the school through the village to the church and place flowers on each grave, and a service is held around the memorial.

After the First World War Harefield Hospital went on to become one of the largest tuberculosis units in the country and then in the Second World War it was again used for war wounded. Now some of the most wonderful heart operations take place there.'

THE SECOND WORLD WAR 1939–1945

Once again, war came to the people of Middlesex and this time the war in the sky affected us all.

▣ THE HOPES OF 1938 ▣

'On the 30th September 1938, my family had just listened on the radio to the Prime Minister, Mr Neville Chamberlain, speaking from Heston airport and reading the declaration which Hitler had signed that morning in Munich which stated that it was "...the desire of our two peoples never to go to war with one another again." The commentator stated that Mr Chamberlain and Lord Halifax would be returning to Downing Street via the Great West Road, and my father suggested that we should take the five minute walk from our house in Isleworth to the Great West Road to see them drive past. This we did, and joined the groups of people who had also come to wave and clap as they drove by with the piece of paper Chamberlain later waved at the crowd in Downing Street when he said: "This is the second time in our

The parade going by on the corner on Eastcote Lane, Northolt, opposite the post office.

history that there has come back from Germany to Downing Street peace with honour. I believe it is peace in our time." How relieved we all were, only to be disillusioned when in less than a year the same Prime Minister would tell us on 3rd September 1939 at 11.15 am "…that we are now at war with Germany."'

❖ THE AIR RAID SHELTERS ❖

'At the outset of the war in 1939 each house had the choice of either a Morrison shelter, which was an indoors one, shaped like a table but made of iron and you slept under it on a mattress with bedclothes, or an Anderson shelter which was erected in the garden, of corrugated iron and which looked like a shed.

My father opted for the Anderson shelter, and he and my two brothers set about erecting it. First of all they made a large hole in our garden at Hayes, about six to eight foot square, lined it with cement and placed the shelter above it. As my father worked on the railway he was allowed to buy used railway sleepers as firewood, so he arranged with his manager to have his allocation delivered uncut. These large sleepers were placed around the shelter at the base of the iron sides, and then he and my brothers filled up the gap with earth, as well as up over the top of the structure. In fact, later on my father actually planted seeds over the top and made it into a flower bed.

Inside the shelter we had five bunk beds. My mother and father slept on the left-hand side, my brothers on the right-hand side and, because I was only nine years old and not very big, my bunk went at the toe of the other bunks. During the bombing of London which went on for many months, during 1940/41, we slept in the shelter every night. We had an oil lamp for reading by, and we even had a wind-up gramophone and records to drown out the sounds of the guns and aeroplanes droning overhead. My mother cut sandwiches, prepared a tray with cups, saucers, milk and sugar, filled thermos flasks with hot water, and took these down the shelter with us for supper. After the raids had stopped for some weeks Father decided that we could once more sleep in the house, but for several nights we were all very nervous.

After the war the shelter was moved to the bottom of the garden and used as a tool shed. My father brought himself a greenhouse and this he placed on top of the remaining shelter base, still using the steps that we had during the war to get in and out; thus he could take full advantage of the sunshine through the glass for his plants.'

◙ BOMBS ON SOUTHALL ◙

'Our house had iron railings which were taken away for the war effort. During the Battle of Britain bombs were dropped on Southall, the Germans apparently aiming for the big factory of AEC Ltd who made army lorries. They missed, and the bombs fell in the park and along the Broadway.'

◙ THE BOMBING OF FAIREY AVIATION ◙

'One afternoon of my childhood, over 50 years ago, still stands out vividly in my memory. It was a summer's day of either 1941 or 1942 when sitting in class at Townfield Senior Girls School there was a terrific bang, all the building and windows shook and the teacher looked at us children horrified. No warning had been sounded but everyone knew that a large bomb had been exploded close by. The teacher made us form up into lines and we quickly marched out of the class room, out into the playground and then on into the shelter. After we had been in the shelter for about half an hour the all clear siren sounded. The word was passed from teacher to teacher that all the classes were allowed to go home immediately. Every girl in my class thought that this was great, an afternoon off school in the sunshine.

As we were walking along Coldharbour Lane in Hayes hundreds of cyclists started to appear coming from the direction of local factories and then we realised that something serious had happened. The cyclists were telling everyone as they passed that the Fairey Aviation aircraft factory had had a direct hit. A lone German aircraft had got through the defence system undetected, dropped its bombs and had also machine gunned pedestrians walking along Hayes station bridge.

On hearing this news I did not feel very happy as both my elder brothers worked at the aircraft factory and my father was a ticket collector with the Great Western Railway at Hayes station and all three were at work at this time. I ran home quickly to tell my mother. I think the next hour or so were the longest I have ever known waiting for news.

My brothers' friend was the first to appear, he had been sent on ahead to let us know that they were both safe but were staying behind to help clear up the mess and to help those who were injured and suffering from shock. There was only one fatality that afternoon. This friend had also seen my father, who was a keen first aider, on Hayes station bridge looking after the wounded until proper medical care could be given. This friend then went on his journey spreading the good news to other families who were still waiting.'

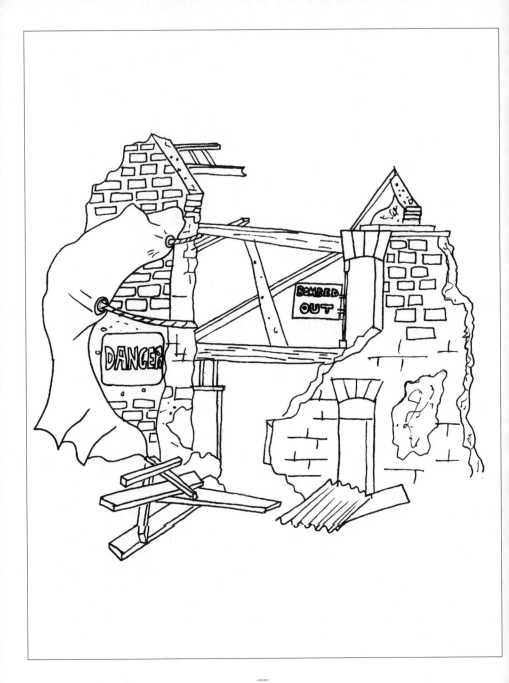

◈ TWO FIELDS FROM NORTHOLT ◈

'When I started at Breakspear School, Ickenham in the 1940s the Germans were still bombing us as we were only two fields away from Northolt airfield. They certainly dropped a few thousand incendiary bombs around the estate where we lived. My two brothers used to go out and collect the used shells as soon as the all clear went and bring them back and build them into a wall in the back garden.'

◈ AN ENORMOUS EXPLOSION IN STAINES ◈

'One of my most vivid memories of the war was in 1944 when a high explosive bomb dropped on Stainash Crescent, about ten minutes walk from Farm Road in Staines.

We heard guns and aircraft very soon after the siren had sounded and Mother decided we should take cover under the stairs rather than walking the length of the garden to the Anderson shelter. My mother, three children and a dog huddled together in the small cupboard, heads bent so as not to hit them on the understairs, prepared to wait until it was quieter and we could get to the shelter for the night.

Suddenly there was an enormous explosion, it sounded like hundreds of claps of thunder all happening at the same time, and my young sister wee'd over the floor. There was the sound of breaking glass, the cupboard door shook and the windows at the back of the house were blown in. The force of the blast had thrown the catch of the door into a locking position, we were trapped. I can't remember how long for, but it seemed hours before my father, ashen faced, opened the door.

He had pushed his cycle through the ambulances, fire engines, police and devastation to get home from work, made doubly distressing because we knew many people in the Crescent and the shopping parade.

I remember how awful I felt when next morning we walked over the rubble, hoping to see friends' front doors still standing. Four people were killed and 17 injured; none were our close friends, but suddenly I really understood what War meant.'

❖ Viola Avenue at War ❖

'Horror came from the skies on the night of Wednesday 23rd February 1944, when high speed Luftwaffe fighter-bombers strafed the area around Stanwell, along a line cutting straight across Egham, Staines, Ashford and Stanwell.

The raid was so quick there was no time to sound a warning. Ten people were killed across the district, four of them in Viola Avenue, Stanwell. Several houses were blown apart as occupants slept. Emergency teams and residents recovered the bodies from beneath the piles of rubble. It was the first time that women ambulance drivers found themselves in the front line.

Until they found other accommodation, the homeless survivors were put up in the village hall. The task was organised by Miss Maisie Webster, and when they were to leave, the people asked her to be in the hall. They pulled the stage curtains back and there was a brand new bicycle they had bought for her.'

❖ Hooters and Flying Bombs ❖

'I was nine years old when the war started. The children in Hayes did not have to be evacuated, but those in Greenford, just over the border, were.

The Gram (HMV) hooter was our siren, not a "moaning Minnie" but just long and short blasts for the warning and the all clear. Our school was closed until the shelters were built. When we did go back, our domestic science classes in particular suffered in the air raids – pearl barley stew boiled dry and we had very well baked bread.

When I was 14 in 1944 I started work for a Hayes printer as a trainee bookbinder, at 17s 6d a week. Walking to work one morning, I saw planes flying in formation overhead. Later that day we heard that the Allies had landed in Europe – it was D-Day. Another morning when we arrived at work we were sent straight to the shelter as a new weapon was being used, the flying bomb. A few weeks later, walking to work, I saw a flying bomb go overhead. Its tail fire went out but I knew I was safe as it had passed over me. It landed in Hillingdon. Another time when we were working bombs started dropping nearby; one hit

the Gram shelter, causing great loss of life. A memorial to those who lost their lives there can be seen in Cherry Lane cemetery, Harlington.

I was very lucky as in all the war I only spent three nights in a shelter (I could sleep through anything). I have been bounced out of bed when a V2 rocket landed on the Food Office in the Uxbridge Road. I have walked home from the cinema with shrapnel falling around me. I have stood in the Uxbridge Road, during the blitz, and watched London burning, the flames reflected in the sky. And, one Sunday morning, I was machine gunned by a German plane.'

▨ ENEMY AIRCRAFT OVERHEAD ▨

'Lunchtime concerts at the National Gallery were well attended (coffee and sandwiches available). It was comforting to listen to Bach's Brandenburg Concertos, or Myra Hess playing Chopin, surrounded by other music lovers, enjoying such remnants of sanity still existing in this mad world.

It was not so funny sitting in the 6.16 waiting to pull out of Paddington (fast to West Drayton) when the station announcer said: "Enemy aircraft overhead, go to shelter immediately." Nobody batted an eyelid, just gripped the newspaper more firmly and prayed for the minute hand on the large double clock to drop more quickly.

On VE Day a celebration £5 was paid to each and every one in

165

my office (shorthand typists were earning about £6 per week in those days) and again on VJ Day we received the same.'

LIFE GOES ON

*W*hatever the year brought, life went on and families had to be fed and clothed. We got used to seeing prisoners of war and coping with rationing and 'make do and mend', and managed to enjoy ourselves as well.

◈ NORTHOLT PIGS AND PRISONERS ◈

'In September 1939 we had already been issued with identity cards and gas masks and ration books soon followed. Part of Kensington playing fields was an army camp and we could hear the bugle calls from our house. There was an anti-aircraft gun at the top of the hill overlooking Northolt aerodrome and we soon learned to distinguish its sound from that of falling bombs.

When out shopping one day my grandmother had to run behind the Hare and Hounds in Greenford when a German plane, having dropped its bombs, used a machine gun to strafe shoppers in the street.

There was a thriving pig club in Northolt. In return for providing meat to go into the normal retail market members were allowed to keep an extra animal to distribute among themselves off ration. They usually managed to rear additional animals that the authorities knew nothing about and these were cut up and distributed on the black market in the area. This was illegal and on one occasion the local carrier was distributing his illicit pig meat by means of his horse and cart when he was stopped by a policeman. The carrier was relieved to find he was looking for a deserter and with great presence of mind told him he thought he had seen someone lurking in a nearby stableyard. The policeman cycled quickly off to investigate and the pork continued on its journey.

When the war ended I was in my teens and we would spend some of our time on the abandoned British Gaumont film studios which stood between Islip Manor Road and Northolt aerodrome. The site consisted of laid out streets with Belisha crossings which had been used for film sets.

German prisoners of war were being used to clear timber from a site at the junction of Ealing Road (now Kensington Road) and Ruislip Road prior to the erection of pre-fabs (which still remain). One day on my way to school I was whistled at by one of the prisoners who was not much older than I was and I remember being angry about it for days afterwards.'

▣ A WARTIME WEDDING IN CHISWICK ▣

'During her wedding, my neighbour Frances tells me, she wouldn't have been surprised to turn round and see all the guests rise from their pews, clutching their smart hats, and disappear towards underground bolt-holes, while she, her bridegroom John, and the vicar stayed to complete the service. But she was lucky. The air raid sirens didn't sound. The wedding party duly went on to cross the road from St Paul's church in Grove Park, Chiswick, to Frances's home, to enjoy the cake (made with fruit saved for months from the family's rations), and to admire the bride's and bridesmaid's dresses (for which John's sister had somehow collected enough clothing coupons).

"Wartime weddings were a bit different," says Frances, casting her mind back to 27th August 1940. "We'd been engaged for a year and it was the first time John got leave from the army. He was in Northamptonshire and I was teaching in Isleworth. So we had to get married then. The trouble was that the real bombing of London had just started. There was a landmine a few streets away the day before. They used to bomb the docks and then come up the river at night, so no one got any sleep." Frances's parents had gone to the country for some rest and came back just for the wedding.

I was in Middlesex too at the time, doing basic WRNS training at Mill Hill, and later in what was rather oddly called "WRNS Isolated Units" – we never felt very isolated in central London –

Frances and John Eldridge leaving St Paul's church, Chiswick in August 1940 – wartime weddings posed problems for some couples.

in quarters on Chelsea Embankment. As German linguists we were assigned to SHAEF (General Eisenhower's Supreme Headquarters Allied Expeditionary Force), on the top floor of Peter Robinson's, and subsequently to Admiralty, where on the way to our offices we used to pass a door intriguingly labelled "Vice Controller". It was another 20 years before I came to live in Chiswick.

Frances already knew about raids because she can remember the Germans bombing Brentford gasworks in the First World War. All the lamps and fires suddenly went out and four year old Frances and her brother, to their astonishment, were whisked down to the coal cellar for safety.

In 1940 St Paul's church still had its stained glass windows (soon to be shattered) and was surrounded by quiet countrified roads. The big Victorian villas which stood at each end of Grove Park Road would soon be destroyed by bombs; and another casualty was the newsagent's shop beside the nearby railway line, where the newsagent's daughter was killed.

They went to Stratford-on-Avon on honeymoon. Frances says, "We found that every hotel had been commandeered by the RAF. Must we sleep under a hedge, we thought? We called at a baker's shop and the people recommended the Cyclist Touring Club House next to the police station. We took the room. As soon as we got into bed, the siren went. But we decided to stay put."

Back in Chiswick, the weather was still hot, so before John went back to his unit they went for a swim in the open air baths. "John got into the water and I was ready to go in when the siren went. Everybody had to get out because there was a dogfight right overhead. It was part of the Battle of Britain."

Many people had Anderson shelters in their gardens; some are still there. Frances's neighbour had a table shelter – "like a sort of reinforced dining table you got under. And there was a big cellar at the wine merchants – everyone went there, and I used to take all my new crockery and precious wedding presents."

Teachers were working eight-hour shifts, and transport was disrupted, so Frances moved to a flat next to the school in Isleworth. Sometimes she visited John – "and I used to hate the long walk back from Osterley station in the blackout, everything pitch dark except for the flashes and the ear-splitting bangs from the ack-ack guns in Osterley Park." One night she found her flat was wrecked – a bomb close by had blown the shutters in. "Never mind, dear," said the two old ladies downstairs, "you can come and live in the cellar with us."

She did for a time, and then moved to a school away from London. John went to Greece and was taken prisoner in 1941. The family house was requisitioned, first for the army, then to house Italian prisoners. It was 1950 before John and Frances got it back, and in due course raised two sons there – who sang in the choir of the church across the road.

To bring off a proper white wedding in Chiswick in 1940 was a kind of personal triumph over the Luftwaffe. You've only to look at Frances's expression in the wedding photo she showed me to know who was winning: and it wasn't Hitler.'

❖ A REFUGE FROM WAR – THE PEGGY BEDFORD ❖

'The Peggy Bedford inn was opened in 1930; it stood at the junction of the Bath Road and Colnbrook by-pass. Whilst other buildings were being pulled down, in order to make way for Heathrow Airport, this mock-Tudor pub remained. Sadly it has now gone, demolished in 1995.

During the war, Miss S. was the licensee of the "Peggy", where she reigned until well into the 1950s. She was a somewhat eccentric character who was passionate about trees and wild-life. When I was about twelve years old, my parents had some visitors and they decided to go to the Peggy for a drink. Rather than leave me in an empty house, they took me along with them. Miss S. took one look at me and said, "I can't allow her in the bar, she can wait in the dining room." This proved to be a long, wide room with a table in the middle, surrounded by high-backed Victorian chairs, and there I sat in solitary confinement with an arrowroot biscuit and a glass of lemonade. Then I spotted an old fashioned coat and hat stand, on top of which I saw a stuffed owl, so I thought, but suddenly the owl moved its head and I was terrified. I learned, later, that Miss S. had rescued the owl and decided to care for it, feeding it on a diet of small rodents.

Years later, the dining room was converted into an attractive cocktail bar with an area for dancing. By this time I was a young woman, single and fancy free. It was St Valentine's day and there was to be a dance at the Peggy. A friend invited me to join her on a blind date, so off we set to the dance. My so called "date" took one look at me, decided I wasn't right (too tall) and thereafter practically ignored me. However, the man organising the dance had taken note, he came to my rescue and has been there ever since.

The Peggy Bedford played an important role in the lives of all local residents during the war, providing refuge from the problems of war.'

▧ THE TIMBER STORES ▧

'In the early 1940s a lot of trees that had been sawn down and cut into planks were stored at Bulls Bridge, Southall for coffins to be used for soldiers' burials after the war had ended. Also at Bulls Bridge was a depot for narrow boats to lay over while waiting for their next cargo. These boats were quite a sight as they use to lay side by side and the bargee and his family had to cross over the outside boats to reach the centre ones. During this time the children of the bargees attended school in Norwood Green, this and perhaps a week or so at their destination whilst awaiting a return cargo, was the only schooling these children received. At the Top Locks on the Grand Union Canal was a cafe. These locks on the canal were just long and wide enough to hold two narrow boats side by side at a time, approximately twelve to fourteen feet long. After the war the British Waterways based their headquarters at Bulls Bridge Wharf, Southall Lane, Southall.'

▧ FARING BETTER IN A VILLAGE ▧

'In 1940 I moved into a house at Hampton. As I was married, I was not called up for the forces but was expected to find a job in a reserved occupation, ie a firm or factory doing work connected with the war. I worked in the boatyard of the Hampton Launch Works on the island of Hampton. High speed air-sea rescue boats and motor torpedo boats were built there. At first there was no bridge and we went across by ferry boats, a climb down or a climb up according to the level of the water. I was very relieved when they built a pedestrian bridge.

Apart from me it was young girls or men over the age of call-up. One man was over 80 and cycled in all weathers from Molesey and came across on the ferry from that side. Some of the desks were of the high type where one sat on high stools, just like in Dickens' time.

The American forces were stationed on Hurst Park racecourse and the young girls were forever out on the balcony waving to them until brought back by the head of the office. I do not know if it was the actual band or records but the music of Glenn Miller came across all day.

A new canteen was built and we could get a lunch there and save our food coupons. Also there was a British restaurant by Hampton station where one could get a very basic meal which once again saved our coupons. As you can see, if one worked full-time one was better off than those with young children who had to provide all meals at home. Also they must have been very lonely in the evenings. I was able to go out visiting. "Workers' Playtime" was when various entertainers all over the country entertained the work people in their lunch-hour.

There were queues for some foods but on the whole we had a very healthy but not varied diet. I am sure being in a small village I fared better than those in the towns. The local shops knew if we worked full-time we could not queue so these foods were added to our orders when they were delivered. As I came home from work, about once a week, there was a parcel of fish waiting for me. The meat ration was 1s 2d and I usually had a piece of best end of lamb. Two of the cutlets I grilled, the rest went in a stew. I grew most of my own vegetables and bottled a lot of tomatoes. I do not think sausages or offal were rationed but were not widely available.

We were only allowed a glimmer of light from our bicycle

lamps and it was difficult riding in the fog. We longed for the full moon so we could get about, but conversely dreaded it too as the air raids came then.

Clothes rationing was very strict and we had to be ingenious to spin our coupons out. I had a winter coat made from a grey blanket and underwear made from parachute silk. Knitting wool was available but we were unable to buy very much owing to the shortage of our coupons. In 1945 when my daughter was born I made dresses for her out of parachute silk and very lovely they were.

GIs were stationed in Bushey Park and billeted all over Hampton. They only had to be provided with a bed and had all their meals in the camp so people were quite glad of the income. The GIs got rather a bad name, mostly through jealousy, as they were paid more than our troops and the girls liked to go out with them.

When my husband came home on a 24 hour pass, in order to spend as much time as possible with him, I used to go to one of the mainline stations to see him off. I would come back on my own in the underground, on the train from Waterloo to Hampton (only a glimmer of light in single compartments) and walk from the station in the blackout and I was not afraid. What a difference to nowadays. If there was an air raid one took shelter if available, otherwise one kept walking. I did fire watching duty in our road, which meant I slept in trousers and sweater. Sunday afternoons, I chanced there being a raid, had a bath and got into bed for a couple of hours.'

◼ LODGERS AND PRISONERS AT HAYES ◼

'All families with husbands away fighting had to take in Irish male lodgers. Our house was allocated two. Mum had to double up with my sister and me, and my brother had the small boxroom and the lodgers had the second bedroom. You had no choice. It was all to help the war effort. Some of these Irish workers were employed on clearing bomb damaged buildings in and around London.

Young German prisoners of war, aged from about 17 to 22,

worked on laying Judge Heath Lane, from where the Hayes Stadium now is down to Barra Hall Circus, that straight stretch of white road. I can remember as a child watching them, wielding their pickaxes and shovels to turn the field and waste land into this very straight road. It was never confirmed officially, but it was said that the road was made extra strong for emergency aircraft landing from Northolt airport. I can still see in my mind's eye those cement mixers pouring in the white cement, and believe that it was very thick.

One day my mother took me shopping to the Uxbridge Road, where we had to cross the fields where the prisoners of war were working. On the way home Mum had bought one dozen penny buns, if you bought a dozen you got one free (this was known as a baker's dozen). She took pity on those young prisoners and threw them all a bun each. She said she only hoped that some one would take care of our prisoners of war in the same situation!

One very nasty incident was the bomb that fell on one of the EMI air raid shelters, a direct hit that killed an awful lot of people. They say some were never found. My mother was in one of the other shelters, thank God. All mothers of children at school had to work so many hours a day or week on war work.'

▣ CYCLING TO WORK ▣

'I left school at the age of 16 in October 1939 and started work at the Air Ministry in Harefield, a month after the outbreak of the Second World War. As I lived in Eastcote the best means of travelling there by public transport was by train to Uxbridge, then a short walk to Manor Way, on a council housing estate at the edge of town, where the bus to Harefield had its terminus. There followed a winter of tedious travel often delayed by snow and ice until in the spring I acquired a bicycle. Then I was able to go a direct route to Harefield via Ruislip for three miles where there was glorious Green Belt country.

Breakspeare Road wound its way, lined with trees, past fields of cows and farms with horses, pigs and chickens. One was

174

conscious of the mighty elms alongside, particularly on the hill going down into the valley before one ascended the rather steep hill into Harefield, and one could see a double line of elms going across the fields forming a "ride" from the big house to Northwood.

A camaraderie was formed with the various cyclists and one was seldom alone. All, if they were sensible, had to dismount for the last few yards of the hill. There were few cars and soon one learned where all the potholes and bends were for some nights were really dark and remember a bicycle lamp had to have half its light restricted because of blackout rules. We coped with wind and rain, frost and fog, sun and snow. I remember leading a car one foggy night whose driver could not see anything beyond me and my bike.

We worked long hours with an early start, and double summer time. I was convinced that I heard a nightingale from Mad Bess Wood many times.

A searchlight station manned by the ATS was situated in the valley opposite to Bowne Farm. V1s, or doodlebugs as they were called, became a hazard and both Bowne Farm and Warren Farm were damaged. We cyclists decided that Breakspeare Road was in a direct line followed by these machines and for one day we pedalled another longer way. The extra mileage soon made us change our minds. Then came the time when Bayhurst Wood seemed to be full of American soldiers and soon after that we were out on the lawn in Harefield watching all the planes going over as it was D-Day (6th June 1944).'

▨ ALONG THE BATH ROAD ▨

'My father had a butcher's shop along the Bath Road near the Sipson Road junction from 1927 to 1950. I am sure when he first opened the shop he must have had a difficult time as it was in the depression. In those days it was a market gardening area and Heathrow Airport had not been built but there was a very small aerodrome at Heathrow used by the Fairey Aviation Company. My first memories of aircraft were the Fairey Aviation Company biplanes flying overhead. Compared to the planes that fly today, they sounded very fragile.

During the war we were issued with ration books and after school I would help my parents count the coupons that had to be sent to the Food Office at West Drayton. We had to account for the amount of meat that was sold in the shop. We were often plagued with air raids at night. When the sirens went, we grabbed our clothes and fled to the Anderson shelter in the garden. We would see the searchlights and hear the anti-aircraft guns and the German bombers overhead. I remember during one air raid I had to run to fetch the midwife when one of my brothers was born. Every household had to buy special blackout curtains and my father was in the Home Guard and had to check all the nearby houses. My two eldest brothers were eventually conscripted into the Army. Peter went to Singapore and Tom to Egypt. Towards D-Day I remember continuous columns of army trucks full of soldiers and military vehicles along the Bath Road heading for the south coast for the invasion of France. The solders were of every nationality – Canadian, American, Australian, South African, Polish etc. Everyone was in uniform.

On VE Day I went to London and joined the crowd outside Buckingham Palace. When the Royal Family appeared on the balcony everyone sang "God save the King". Finally war was over and there was great jubilation, the roar of a London crowd is something I shall never forget.'

▣ LIFE AT THE JOLLY GARDENERS, CRANFORD ▣

'On 15th May 1941 my parents, sister and I moved from London to the Jolly Gardeners, High Street, Cranford, which was licensed to sell beer and tobacco. Dad left London before us in order to be at Brentford County Court for the changeover of the licence to sell beer from the previous landlady.

Peg, Mum and I together with Oscar our cat (travelling in a zipper bag, with opening for air) travelled by two buses to reach Finsbury Park tube station, then on the Piccadilly Line tube train all the way to Hounslow West. We got out and caught another

The Jolly Gardeners pub at Cranford, on the left of the street.

bus to Bath Road, Cranford and then walked one mile to
Cranford village.

It was a lovely sunny day and eventually we came to the army
pillbox, then the Lilian Gardener almshouses beautifully
situated among old established trees and then curving round the
cottages called "The Crescent", we saw our new home.

It was a long yellow brick building with a slate roof and whose
front elevation was level with the pavement. Lifting up the latch
of the heavy front door you entered the front bar. The room was
of medium size and immediately opposite was a counter
approximately four feet wide with a half door underneath. The
floor was covered with brown cork lino and the walls were lined
with wooden wheelback chairs and in the corners similar larger
chairs with arms. There was also a scrubbed wooden table. There
was no heat in this bar but eventually Dad was able to install a
gas fired radiator that did not need a flue.

In the wall to the left of the front door was another door that led into the main bar, "the tap room". Under the window were long wooden benches for sitting and a shorter one just behind the door. In the centre of the room was a scrubbed wooden table with scrubbed wooden benches on either side where the customers sat to play dominoes and cribbage. The outside wall was clear of benches as this area was for playing darts on the board which hung in the alcove to the left of the open coal fire. To the right of the fireplace was a short wooden bench hard up against the small hatchway where the drinks were served. One of our regular customers used to sit there every night and drink his way through seven pints of ale. He seldom moved from his seat and we often joked that he must have had a spare tank somewhere. At 10.15 each evening he used to ask for a half pint bottle of stout for "the missus" and then he used to toddle home.

A long corridor ran from the serving area to the back door with two living rooms off to the left and to the right were the stairs to the upper floor and then the door to the cellar which was four brick steps below ground level. All the barrels of ale, bitter and old ale, together with the bottled beer and mineral waters were stored in the cellar so every order had to be brought up from the cellar and the beer was drawn direct "from the wood" through brass taps. The cellar was stone floored and with a small barred window high up on the outside wall. There was a wide door on the outside wall and a wooden platform on which the barrels were rolled into the cellar from the brewer's vehicle and then they were rolled into position on their stands and had to settle for 48 hours before the beer was clear to serve. On the wooden platform during opening hours was kept an enamelled iron bowl with cold water in it for rinsing glasses and these were then left to drain on enamelled iron trays. The cellar was a very cold place. The whole house was gas lit.

Upstairs were four bedrooms and a long attic whose ceiling sloped right down to floor level. We used this room for storage but rumour had it that the previous landlords who also were market gardeners sometimes used this room for sleeping accommodation for field workers.

We had a very large uncultivated garden with a high brick wall at the end of it and a lower brick wall to one side. In the far corner were the remains of stables with sagging roofs and the feeding troughs and chains still attached to this wall.

On the other side of the High Street at the end of the cottage gardens was the perimeter fence of Heston airport. During the war it was a fighter station and Spitfires operated from there. They used to scream up in to the sky in their threes right over the roof of the pub. One day just after midday a fighter pilot came in to land too low and crashed into the field at the back of our garden, narrowly missing the brick wall, and the plane flipped over in the green hedge. By chance at the same time a coachload of RAF men were going along the High Street on their way to lunch. The coach stopped and there was the sound of flying boots as the boys rushed up the lane and through the field gate and they got their comrade out of the plane with the help of an axe Dad lent them. They gave him a chair lift and carried him to the coach. We later heard that he had damaged an ankle in the crash. A guard was placed on the plane and eventually it was taken away on an RAF transporter.

In August 1944 Mum had another baby and during the afternoon Dad and I cycled through the back lanes to Harlington and Sipson cottage hospital to see them. Whilst we were going along Sipson Lane we heard a doodle bug so we jumped off our bikes and crouched in the ditch until it had gone over. Later Mum used to tell us how when the sirens sounded, their very smart modern Matron used to rush into the seven-bedded ward and tell the mums to lie flat in their beds. She then used to pull the black iron bed tables over the heads and upper bodies of the patients and then the mums would hear her high heels clattering along the stone corridor en route to the Anderson shelter in the hospital's garden.

In recent years the Jolly Gardeners has been modernized but I am very glad that I lived there when it was still the way it had been designed.'

▣ THE AGE OF CHIVALRY IS DEAD! ▣

'When I was 13 I knitted garments for the Forces and they were distributed by Prices Patent Candle Company, for whom my aunt worked. All garments were distributed with the name and address of the knitter, so you can imagine how thrilled I was, at that age, to receive a letter from Scotland, from an Alan Davidson who had received my pullover. He thanked me very much and said that he was sure I would make a good wife to someone one day. I have now been married for 44 years, but I do not know whether my knitting was my biggest asset!

During my early working life, I worked in London in Bloomsbury for a chartered quantity surveyor. To save time I suggested I went out with the surveyors to take details of buildings which had been requisitioned – this saved them writing it all down and then dictating it to me back in the office. One day, in the era of the doodlebugs, we were in Mayfair at a very grand house. We had finished all the rooms inside, and then went up on to the roof. At that moment a doodlebug appeared in the distance – sun shining to make it look like a flying cross. I turned to the surveyor to remark how "pretty" it looked, and to my astonishment I found I was alone. He had gone down the ladder as fast as he could and left me up there alone – my earliest lesson on whether the age of chivalry was dead!'

DOING OUR BIT

On the Home Front we all did our bit, whether as air raid wardens or in the Land Army, or simply by offering a helping hand to those in need.

▣ IN THE ARP ▣

'In the early 1940s I was being "courted" by my husband-to-be. We were in our teens and lived in Acton. We were members of the youth club and he was often around our house, going to the club, for walks, the pictures or perhaps a local hop – we loved dancing. They were the usual type of activities for our age group in wartime. I had to be home by 10 to 10.30 pm on weekdays, 11 pm on Saturdays.

Frank was an ARP messenger, no walkie-talkies in those days. About a dozen or so young men, before being called up to the services, used to take messages from headquarters, Acton Town Hall, to the various air raid incidents occurring in the area.

On this particular evening the warning siren sounded so he got on his bike, borrowing my Dad's tin hat as it was already very noisy with guns going (Big Bertha nearby) and bombs falling, and off he went to the town hall.

Next day he returned Dad's tin hat and told us how he got on. Apparently he had begun to cycle quickly and it sounded as though a bomb was following him – the faster he pedalled the more it seemed to chase him. It turned out to be the airholes each side of Dad's hat and the "bomb" was the wind rushing through them – a frightening experience. We had a good laugh of course. We took it for granted that these lads, under 18 years of age, were doing their bit and in the thick of it before even being called to active service.'

In the summer of 1939 my husband and I decided to train as air raid wardens as a modest contribution towards the war effort. There was a feeling of unusual satisfaction as we crawled on the dirty floor of the old fire station, battling with imaginary smoke and flames; or gathered round the ambulance for first aid practice on Saturday mornings. One young volunteer as the patient, his arm in a sling and legs in splints, was pushed triumphantly into the ambulance, the doors slammed, and he arrived at the hospital with an all too genuine broken nose. At the end of the course we were given a certificate and required to join the rota of night-shifts. We set out as it grew dark for the basement of a men's college at the top of the hill. Six camp beds, army blankets and a kettle kept us sleeping spasmodically until dawn. Then, one Sunday morning came the great moment. The air raid siren sounded just as it was growing light. Panic. Which way round with the yellow oilskin capes and tin helmets? On with the armband, gas mask and whistle, and, clasping the rattle and note pad, we strode boldly forth into the cloudless sky of a beautiful summer morning.

Our beat was along the length of the Terrace at Richmond with its glittering view down through the fields to the Thames. Not a soul was in sight, nothing and nobody stirring – not a sound – until my husband, always a stickler for regulations, blew his whistle loudly several times and rattled his rattle for good measure. I have never been so embarrassed. It somehow seemed sacrilegious. I clung to his arms to stop him. We waited tensely, irrationally hoping no one had heard. But the silence, the sun and the view were still there as we dissolved into helpless laughter, and continued our incongruous way as the all clear sounded.'

'Perhaps I should tell the story of my father who was an air raid warden in Ealing. One foggy November night he mistook his way across Walpole Park and walked straight into the stagnant duck pond. He was, of course, complete with heavy uniform and gas mask and sank. He eventually returned home where my mother refused to let him in. The pond had not been cleaned for years and he reeked. He left his clothes in the garden and came in for a bath but he was very miserable. He had left his pipe and tobacco in the duck pond.'

▣ KEEPING IN TOUCH ▣

'On the Railway Estate in Hayes they had an association called the Hayes Garden Village Tenants' Association. They even had their own benevolent fund to call upon when they were off work sick and not receiving pay.

At the beginning of the war some of the husbands, sons and daughters were called up to serve in the forces, land army, etc. The management committee of the estate came up with the idea that they would keep in contact with these men and women.

Every rent day one of the committee members would sit in the rent hut with a box and when the tenants came to pay their rent they would put any spare coppers they could afford into the tin. The committee then went to the local tobacconist and bought packets of cigarettes, and for those who didn't smoke, bars of chocolate. They then went around the estate and collected the names and addresses of all the men and women who had left home.

My father was the secretary of the association and I can remember him sitting up, late into the night, packing up packets of cigarettes and bars of chocolate and with each one he would put a letter in to let the husband and children know how their wives and parents were getting on. I know that this was very much appreciated because the boys and girls would write and thank him and each letter that he received was put on the notice board in the rent hut so that the tenants could read them. Unfortunately, as time went on cigarettes became scarce, sweets were rationed and so many youngsters were being called up that the wives, who were left at home on their own, couldn't afford to even spare a few coppers because they had their children to look after. My father who was over call-up age, took this as being part of his war effort and kept in touch with some of the boys throughout the rest of the war.

His other war effort task he set himself was being an air raid warden and every evening when he was not on late shift (he worked for the Great Western Railway as a guard) he would patrol the estate and if the siren had already sounded his main task was to see that the wives with young children living on their own, were safely in their shelters, or tucked up in whichever cupboard they felt safest in, under the stairs or in the converted coal cellar. Often the children were frightened and crying, especially if the guns sounded heavier than usual, and he would stay with them until they had quietened down and gone to sleep.

My mother would also visit these ladies during the daytime to see if they needed any assistance, even looking after the young children while their mother did her shopping, especially if the kiddies were sick or a little off colour.'

183

◼ AT ICI YEADING ◼

'During the war my mother and her best friend were conscripted to work at the ICI Yeading ammunition factory. Because my mother still had me at school she only had to work afternoons, but because her friend had no young family she had to work full time.

One particular afternoon the air raid warning had sounded so all the women had to take to the shelters. Suddenly they heard machine gun fire. My mother, who was always inquisitive at the best of times, came out of the shelter to see what was happening and there were two fighter planes having a dog-fight in the air.

As she turned round to go back into the shelter she noticed that there was a shed quite close. As I said, my mother was always inquisitive and she decided to go over and see what was stored there. You can imagine her surprise when she found that it was live ammunition that had been packed into boxes and stored ready for despatch. She told us that if a bomb had dropped on the shed the women in the shelter would not have stood a chance. When they returned to their place of work they pointed this out to their manager, who was as surprised as they were. Luckily he took action and had the ammunition moved to another, safer part of the factory.

At that time the ICI factory covered the whole of the corner across from the White Hart public house, from Willow Tree Lane up to and along the Ruislip Road East. St Joseph the Worker church now stands on the ground together with the two council estates owned by both Ealing Borough and Hillingdon Borough. After the war the factory closed and I believe the ground stood derelict for some years because it needed to be cleared and made safe.

During the war there was a shop in Coldharbour Lane, Hayes that sold horse meat. Horse meat was not rationed. Every week I had to queue up to buy this horrible smelling meat for my mother's forewoman at the ICI factory at Yeading. She said she had a dog as a pet, but she bought so much of it that we wondered whether her family ate it themselves. Some people did to offset their meat ration, and if people liked it, they were glad

184

to do so. I used to hate queuing up at this shop because they always cleaned the window and the marble slabs with an ammonia solution and to this day if I get a whiff of ammonia I immediately get a splitting headache. I am sure it is only reaction, just the same as when I hear a siren sound in a film on television my stomach automatically turns over. I wonder how many other "war children" still get this reaction?'

◙ Helped by the British Legion ◙

'My first association with the British Legion was during the war. My father, who was off work with a long term sickness, did not receive any wages from the Great Western Railway. The only money coming in was ten shillings a week from a sick club he joined and the money my mother earned doing part time war work, which was almost a pittance. As we were in rented accommodation the first priority was, of course, the rent. Luckily we were entitled to cheap coal from the railway to use for heating and cooking, but this left little for food for three people.

As my father had served as a regular Royal Marine, and out of sheer desperation, my mother went along to the British Legion to see if they could help us in any way. You can imagine how thankful we were when they allowed us food vouchers that we took along to the Co-op in Hayes Town to exchange for food each week. Also, because of the nature of my father's illness he required special foods, so they got in touch with the authorities and arranged for him to have extra rations.

I can remember after the war ended in 1945 going with my father to the British Legion offices in Uxbridge Road, next to the Adam and Eve public house where they had two converted houses. About this time my father was the secretary of the local branch and remained so for a number of years. I can remember how excited he became when they started to plan the new building, Legion House on the Uxbridge Road, Hayes. Also when it was eventually opened and he was invited to attend the opening ceremony. My father remained a staunch Legionnaire until the day he died.'

■ Turned to War Purposes ■

'My family's furniture business was in Tottenham, part of the light industry furniture-making belt that stretched up through north-east London. Output was drastically altered during the Second World War. From making elaborate dining room furniture we turned to Utility dining rooms – simple in style and all the better for it.

The major part of production was turned to war purposes – making mine detector cases from the still relatively new material Bakelite, and coffins for GIs. The latter were lined in white nylon and were produced by the hundred; fortunately workers assigned to this production took their jobs light-heartedly, and whistled and sang along with the rest.

Most of the workforce was, naturally, women, and during air raids they were shepherded into a purpose-built shelter large enough to accommodate them all, while the men went into two smaller shelters. At night the women's shelter was transformed into our family home – camp beds made up, carpet unrolled, radio plugged in; electricity and plumbing were laid on. As a small child I much preferred day time air raids, for then I would be petted and made much of by all the women, whereas at night the only amusement was to watch my mother – a poor knitter at the best of times – drop stitches every time a bomb dropped nearby.'

■ A Land Girl at Halliford ■

'I came to Halliford in June 1941, as a land girl at the Halliford French Gardens (now the Squires Garden Centre), so named because they had a French foreman before the war. He specialised in growing crops on hot beds of manure and in cloches (bell-shaped glass) for early cultivation. With the war, it reverted back to the usual way of growing vegetables and salads and Mr Capelen was the foreman.

It was quite rural at that time, with a very limited bus service. We walked to Walton, Laleham and Hampton Court. Halliford Halt railway station was constructed during the war years for

A group of land girls in 1945, just some of those who worked on Middlesex farms and market gardens during the war.

the workers at the nearby British Thermostat factory. Mrs Lane's post office and general shop was the one shop in the village. A mile or so on was a tiny shack which sold various things, owned by Mrs Smeath.

In May 1943, I witnessed a tragic accident. Two of our planes collided and crashed almost over Halliford and parts of the wreckage came down in the Bugle Field.'

A Child's War

Children had to adapt to enormous changes in their lives and to the new fears they faced as air raids continued. Many were evacuated to places of greater safety, or their schooling interrupted by the arrival of evacuees at their own home village.

▨ LESSONS WERE ADAPTED ▨

'I was twelve at the outbreak of war, at the Greenway Senior School in Uxbridge, and lessons had to be adapted to meet the shortages. Cookery was one – due to rationing the teacher only did the cooking with pupils taking notes and watching. When an exercise book was full it was turned upside down and any spare spaces as well as the cover had to be filled before a new exercise book was issued.'

▨ A SOUTHALL CHILD ▨

'I was six when the war started and my schooling was rather disrupted as classes were often held in places other than the school in Beaconsfield Road. We had classes in huts, rooms over shops and even shelters.

Brick-built shelters appeared in roads, including Hambrough Road. We had an Anderson shelter in the back garden and were often woken at night to go and sleep there. When the bombing was bad, we went to sleep there every night. If a night raid had disturbed our sleep too much, we were excused school the next day.

Our lovely metal fence and gate was taken away so that the metal could be used for war weapons. The nearest bomb to us was at the top of Hambrough Road and we only lost a small piece of glass from the porch.

I can remember American servicemen being in Southall which

A surface air raid shelter in Southall.

was very exciting. The children used to go up to them and say "Got any gum, chum?", meaning chewing gum as this was something of a novelty. I never did have the nerve to ask for any. Of course everything was rationed, including sweets.'

◙ SHAKING LIKE A RATTLE ◙
'We lived in Ickenham from 1939. When the sirens went after I was tucked up in bed I would go stiff and shout for Mum or Dad and shake like a rattle. One or the other would take me downstairs, where I would hide under the table.'

◙ THE TERROR I FELT ◙
'I remember the terror I felt the first time we had a gas mask drill, as the sight of the ugly mask filled me with horror. Unknown to the teachers, and indeed my parents, I never did master the art of

putting one on. We carried the masks everywhere with us, and some people even made quite attractive cases for them so that they became almost fashion accessories.

Lessons in wartime were frequently interrupted by air raids, sometimes several in one day. We would have to leave everything immediately and take cover in basement rooms. We thought this was great fun at first, and happily passed the time playing Happy Families, until then staff decided that we each must take an approved book with us, to be followed by discussion on return to the classroom.'

◈ SINGING IN THE SHELTER ◈

'I can remember four types of shelters in the war. The first meant sleeping under Mum and Dad's sagging mattress springs, on the ground floor of the house during the early air raids (I was three years old when war broke out). Then I graduated to a wooden bunk in the new Anderson shelter underground at the end of the back garden (a real adventure).

We would go dodging in and out of the long brick shelters built down our side of the road (Hambrough Road, Southall) on the way to and from school. No parking problems down our road in those days! And finally, there was sitting in a long dug out, covered with soil, at Beaconsfield Road infants and junior school. We sat on benches down the sides. It was like a big Anderson shelter.

Whilst in the shelter we sang songs with Miss Crispen, our teacher. One of them began:

> There's a hole in the bottom of the sea,
> There's a hole in the bottom of the sea,
> There's a hole, there's a hole,
> There's a hole in the bottom of the sea."

Then the second verse continued: "There's a log in the hole in the bottom of the sea," etc, etc. Continue as for the first verse and keep adding things for each verse until you have something like this for the last: "There's a flea, on the hair, on the spot, on the wart, on the frog, on the leaf, on a twig, on a bough, on the branch, on the bump, on the log, in the hole in the bottom of the sea."

I think there were about twelve verses in all, but depending on the length of the air raid I believe our teacher would add more things to the list. It used to puzzle me how the frog balanced on a leaf.'

HIGHDAYS & HOLIDAYS

MUSIC, SPORTS AND CINEMA

Much of our entertainment we made ourselves, and even the smallest village seemed to be able to provide sports and social occasions. Gramophones and then the radio brought music into our homes, but we loved going to the cinema and to the events put on in our local venues, from Wembley Stadium to Kneller Hall.

▣ SOMETHING GOING ON EVERY EVENING! ▣

'Social life at Grange Park, Enfield in the mid 1950s was centred on the two local churches, with clubs and meetings for all ages – the Young Wives' Club, the Mothers' Union, Fellowships etc. The cinema was a popular form of entertainment and Enfield boasted three – the Capitol, the Essoldo and the Florida.'

'Something going on every evening in the 1950s! It seemed that every church in the Cranford and Harlington area had a youth club as well as Guides, Girls' Life Brigade, Boys' Brigade, etc. At Harlington Baptist church there was the Campaigners, an organisation older than Scouts and Guides, which was divided into Juno's for young children, Intermediates and then Craftsmen for the over 14s. Boys and girls, although separated at their meetings, met once a month for Church Parade, in full uniform, to march through Harlington and then to morning service. No Campaigners in Harlington now. The church also had a youth club, complete with a drama group.

In Hounslow, the Treaty Road Undenominational church was the one to attend. They had a youth club meeting every night, Tuesdays and Fridays being popular for games, table tennis especially. A very successful cricket team and the football eleven from this church took part in a local league. By juggling your religious obligations it was possible to lead a very full social life, especially when on the lookout for boyfriends. The girls seemed to be the church attenders and the boys turned up at services just enough to keep their place in sports teams or the club.

If you didn't go to church then there were the cinemas in the Hounslow area to tempt you. The Ambassador at Hounslow West; the Regal and the Alcazar next door to each other at one end of Hounslow High Street; the Dominion at the bus garage end of the High Street and, in the middle of these, the Empire or Flea Pit as it was known. The Empire showed old films and the programme was changed mid-week, so it was possible, if you had a boyfriend who was working, to go to the cinema six nights a week.

No money? Then Cranford Park was available for the local crowd to go to. We rode track bikes and had cycle races, climbed trees, sat in big gangs talking and joking. We didn't harm anyone but dreamed of owning a Claude Butler racing bike, or one of the new transistor radios. Plane spotting became a new interest for some as London Airport took shape. Boys talked of the trepidations they felt at starting out in National Service, and I remember they agreed that the Royal Air Force was the best to go for, so that they could apply for work at the airport afterwards.'

'In the late 1940s Hayes was rich with things to do in your leisure time. There were three cinemas: the Ambassador, Savoy and Corinth. Also we had the Regent Theatre situated where the National Westminster Bank is now. I can remember walking home after a play in thick snow, everyone throwing snowballs as they went along, even people you didn't know joined in. But the time I looked forward to most was going to the Saturday night dance at the Fairey Canteen in Station Road.

It had a live band which was the norm in those days, a local band made up of singer and drums: Roy Busby, the Moore Brothers (famous names in the area now for carpets and furniture) and another person known as "Gabby" because his surname was Gabb. We thought they were terrific. Teenagers came from miles around, some to dance, others just to listen to the music. All the girls dressed up in their taffeta dresses and

195

frilly petticoats, similar to those worn for American square dancing these days, and the boys were dressed in their best suits. We all thought we were the "cat's whiskers". There was no bar so during the interval most people popped out to the nearby cafe on Fairey Corner and if you were not back before ten o'clock the doorman would not let you back in again. Also smoking was not allowed in the Canteen, anyone found doing so was immediately asked to leave, but this very rarely happened.

At this time Wistow House, one of the oldest buildings in Hayes village, was owned by the Fripp family. They had converted a large barn into a dance studio and the son Ernie and daughter Edna gave ballroom dancing lessons there every Tuesday and Thursday night followed by general dancing until ten o'clock, the "witching-hour" in those days. I remember rushing home from work, eating a quick meal and cycling to Church Road so as not to miss the start. They were strict – no jiving was allowed, but all us teenagers loved it.'

▣ THE UP AND COMING THINGS ▣

'In the 1930s a boy could take his girlfriend to the cinema, buy ice cream in the interval, and a fish and chip supper for £1. The Granadas, Astorias and Odeons gave a lot of pleasure to a great many people. I remember queuing up for the first "talkie" *Broadway Melody* and one of the songs the star sang, *You were meant for me.*

My brother's hobby was wireless and in the early days he made our first crystal set. A box contained a peculiar looking, irregular shaped piece of crystal which was suspended at one end. At the other end a piece of wire on a small movable arm called the "cat's whisker" had to be applied in an experimental fashion to the crystal. If we were lucky we would hear through the headphones "2LO calling" and the sound of the Savoy Orpheans delighted our ears – just magic.

Wireless progressed by leaps and bounds and the next set was a three-valve set, which Bertie built at a cost of about £6. It had a high tension (HT) dry battery, 100 volts, which cost about 16s and a high tension accumulator (wet), 100 volts, which cost about 75s and was rechargeable. Then there was a low tension accumulator (wet), two volts, costing 12s and this could be recharged for a shilling per week. A shop-bought set would probably have cost about £12 10s plus £2 or £4 for the loud-speaker, plus the batteries.

At one time my brothers were dirt-track racing enthusiasts; Bertie rode the dirt-track Douglas while Billy was the skilled mechanic who tuned the engine. The Douglas fell out of favour and the next machine was a Rudge Whitworth with a JAP engine. Bertie was being paid £1 appearance money to ride, but the expected fortune seemed far off, and he needed one day off per week for practising. The BBC did not like this and Father told him that he should take care of his new job as "this wireless is the up and coming thing you know."

Both my brothers worked at Savoy Hill, the first British Broad-casting Company, later to become Corporation. Bertie fitted the first recording equipment to the tower at Big Ben to record the Westminster chimes. Only relations were permitted visitors in the studios in those days and when Bertie took me to see Jack Payne's Dance Band, saying I was his sister, the door attendant said, "Ah yes, they all say that." They could take me to the dinner-dance at Motspur Park, their sports club where Bertie played rugby football. I danced with Sir John Reith – I got him in the Paul Jones; a fine handsome man and the scar on his cheek did not detract from his good looks at all.

When the boys became engaged to be married they collected their cutlery from Black Cat cigarette coupons. Carreras Black Cat coupons also provided me with my first camera. Kodak had produced the first box camera for the masses in 1900. The No 2 Box Brownie was a simple and marvellous camera – just back to the sun, point at the object, and click away.

Players cigarettes were ten for sixpence with a coloured card. BDV packets used to include my favourite little silk pictures, and Kensitas issued material squares embroidered in flowers.

Thin green and gold paper envelopes of Willy Woodbines cost only 2d for five. Cigarettes of low quality were referred to as

Gaspers, and some cheeky old chaps used to say "Have another coffin nail" when offering their packet to a friend. My husband told me that in West Sussex Hospital there used to be a notice displayed: "No cure for Woodbine Smokers".

Schoolboys dived on empty cigarette packets in the gutter to see if a card had been left inside. They played a street game which consisted of propping a row of single cards against the garden wall; the contestant at the kerb tried to knock them down, with a sharp flick attack with one of his own cards. The failed cards piled up in front of those still standing and when you did knock one down, you acquired all. Apparently it gave an extra impetus to your flicking if you licked the edge of your attacking card!

By the 1930s, however, there were serious adult collectors of cigarette cards in many series, and the information printed on the back of them was of high quality and accurate. Some big-headed know-alls might be described as having "got it all off the back of cigarette cards."'

◾ A REAL TREAT ◾

'We had jigsaws, snakes and ladders, draughts and dominoes. We played ping pong (table tennis) on the kitchen table. Our dog used to compete for the ball when it went on the floor. We had a wind-up gramophone and played 78 rpm records, such as *Yes, we have no bananas* and danced to polka tunes. Some families sang around their piano, but we did not have one, nor a radio for many years.

I remember going to the Radio Show and seeing Bob Hope and Bing Crosby just before the war. My cousin, now in America and eight years younger, remembers my mother taking us downstairs in a building in, she believes, Oxford Street, London, where we saw one of the first television programmes for free.

We often went walking over the golf links, from which we once saw the Hendon Air Show, and rambled across to Carpenters Park. The weekly show at the Coliseum, Harrow was a real special treat, and especially in the circle at 2s 6d. I recall how Anona Wynn jumped onto the grand piano and danced there.'

☙ ICKENHAM BRIDGE ❧
'Before the First World War the centre of social activities was the Men's Institute room where the men gathered to play a game of cards known as Ickenham Bridge. No one outside that room knew the rules but three exponents of the game were Reg Weeden, Harry Wilden and Sam Saich who always had his favourite chair and woe betide anyone else who sat in it.'

☙ HAYES AND HARLINGTON COMMUNITY CENTRE ❧
'At the beginning of the war a lot of men and women were conscripted into the Hayes area to work in the factories. These people had to live in lodgings. Unfortunately, they often had nowhere to go except to sit in their bedrooms. Some landladies did not like them to do any cooking or washing in their rooms. So this was the reason why the community centre came into being. It was equipped with a laundry where washing could be done, and hung on pulleys which were raised to the ceiling, and the clothes left to dry while the owners were at work. There was a room equipped with ironing boards so that they could press their shirts and dresses before going out. In the lounge there was a large open fire with easy chairs for them to sit and read in comfort. During the war, I understand that they could even get a meal at the centre.

I joined the centre in 1956. The laundry was still there and young men in lodgings still did their washing at the community centre. The ironing was a different story, quite often they would get one of the girls to iron their shirts for them. I can remember ironing seven shirts one evening. The open fireplace and easy chairs were still there, and of an evening the members would sit around the fire in the winter months having a chat. There was a roster as to who would make the cups of tea for which everyone paid. There was no alcohol sold at the centre in those days, if you wanted a drink you crossed the road to the Victoria pub in North Hyde Road, but this only happened occasionally on a Saturday night.

There was also a good reference library at the centre from

which you could borrow books for the evening, you were not allowed to take them away. There was always something going on. Dancing to records on Monday nights, darts another night, table tennis, bridge, chess, and there was always someone to play with. Also we used to go on car and scooter runs (scooters were very popular at the time). There was a tennis section and we played at Pinkwell Park, but the most popular of all was the rambling section when we used to hire a coach on a Sunday, leave the centre at 9 am and often didn't get back until late in the evenings, after stopping off for a meal somewhere. This section used to operate all year round and every time we had a full coach. In June/July we used to go for a midnight ramble. First we would attend a dance at the centre, then change into our rambling gear, board the coach and set off for the Maidenhead or High Wycombe area and start walking at about midnight. Next morning the coach would meet us, generally at the bottom of the hill at West Wycombe in a field, and then we would cook our breakfast. What a lovely smell. Afterwards we would go home to bed.'

◼ FIRST TO HAVE A GRAMOPHONE ◼

'We were the first family in Sipson to have a gramophone, with a horn. We also had a phonograph with the cylinders. I can remember the local children used to stand in our garden to listen. Our favourites were Al Jolson singing *Sonny Boy* and Gracie Fields singing *Sally*. I must have had a very understanding mother and father to allow it.'

◼ MIDDLESEX COUNTY CRICKET CLUB ◼

'In pre-war days my knowledge of our county cricket team was confined to cigarette cards of some of its more famous players; a picture on the front and a potted history on the reverse side. Jim Sims, Walter Robins and Patsy Hendren were heroes but unseen for I had never seen them in action. Indeed, I didn't even know at that time where they played. I had of course heard of Lords but only as a place where Test Matches were played and I had no realization that Middlesex had been playing their home games there since 1877.

Then came the immediate post-war years. No longer did we have "fag cards" but advertising boards everywhere showed the head of the county's favourite son, the Brylcreem Boy, Dennis Compton, whilst daily and evening papers the length of the land were full of the cricketing exploits of the Terrible Twins (Edrich and Compton) and the rest of that wonderful side of 1947 when Middlesex won the first of their many post-war county championships. After that golden summer though the comprehensive cover of county cricket began slowly to decline in many newspapers and with the disappearance of the *Evening Star* and the *Evening News* reports on the doings of Middlesex became less. Then came the era of television and I could now see my modern day heroes, not on a piece of stiff cardboard, but there in front of me and what is more, from the comfort of my own armchair.'

◼ Wembley Stadium ◼

'In the late 1940s, early 1950s, I remember rushing home from London on a Wednesday night, getting changed, and hurrying to catch the coach to Wembley Stadium. I didn't have time to eat a meal so my mother always prepared me sandwiches and a flask of coffee that I could eat and drink in the coach. This was the speedway night and Wembley Lions were our heroes.

All the local coach companies ran special trips to Wembley which you booked in advance; my friends and I booked for the whole season in advance. When you arrived at Wembley there were literally hundreds of coaches despatching their passengers out into the stadium.

The roar of the crowd when the first riders appeared, the thrill of the speed. On one occasion I nearly knocked my sister-in-law down over the terrace I got so excited, and she was pregnant at the time, and when the "Lions" won a heat, and eventually the whole evening's match, the cheering was horrendous.

201

My special hero was Cyril Rogers; he and his brother rode for Exeter City, whom I used to support with my cousins when I was on holiday. The two brothers actually lived in Southall and when they appeared at Wembley then I was in heaven! The Exeter track was more exciting than Wembley because it was a cinder track, banked at both ends, and you stood on the grass bank seats close to the track. Every time the riders went around a corner the bystanders were covered in cinders. We always had to queue up for the bath when we got home.

Speedway always took place in the summer months because it was outside. In winter months we had ice hockey. Once again it was the thrill of the speed. The players would go around the arena at, I swear, 50 mph if not more. The players were generally big, handsome Canadians, made to look even bigger by the amount of padding they had to wear for safety. The team was, once again, known as the "Wembley Lions". Unfortunately, we could only go to this on a Saturday night because it was not so popular as the speedway and the coach companies did not run trips mid-week. We had to make our own way to Wembley from Hayes, but it was well worth it. During the two intervals, the sweepers would come out to clean the ice. This was quite spectacular in itself because there were two rows of sweepers with brushes, about six foot long, brushes touching, and they would start off with short strokes keeping to music, making their way up the arena, first forming a "V" shape, until eventually they met in two rows facing each other. One sweeper at the end of each row would then brush the collected loose ice chippings into a pile and it would be shovelled up and taken away. The crowd would always applaud them.

Also at this time the Pantomimes on ice had begun. What a spectacular evening these were, I remember seeing *Sleeping Beauty* and *Aladdin*, amongst many more.

I have even been to Wembley Stadium to watch football in the past, and the athletics, with so much going on at the same time. Once I even went there for a meal and watched the dog racing at the same time. Unfortunately, as usual, I didn't win.'

◉ KNELLER HALL, TWICKENHAM ◉

'I will always remember my first summer evening concert at Kneller Hall. It was in the mid-1950s. I went along by coach with the Hayes and Harlington Silver Band. As is the norm, the concert was in the open-air. Some of the military bandsmen in their dress uniforms, with instruments shining in the lights, were already on the bandstand and the remaining bands marched out from the trees playing as they came, I never did realise when the marching bands stopped playing and the bands on the bandstand took over. It was a marvellous evening. The memory of the Last Post has always remained with me. As the bands were playing a large glowing firework was let off behind the trees; as the glow died down it looked like the setting sun so the bands played "At the going down of the sun we shall remember". What a sight and what an impression it left. Although I have seen this many times since, that first time is the one I remember most.

Kneller Hall is the Army's Royal School of Music at Twickenham, next door to the famous "Twickers" Rugby Football Stadium. Pupils come from all over the world to learn to play and arrange military music and also to be band leaders.

I also remember my first carol concert held by the Kneller Hall bands and the London Bach Choir in one of the local churches at Twickenham. The atmosphere was beautiful, such music accompanied by wonderful voices.'

◉ EARLY RADIOS ◉

'I was born in Hayes in 1930. We had a wireless that was built by my father. It stood about five feet high, with a huge horn on top. It was full of glass valves, and it also had low and high tension batteries and a glass accumulator. The accumulator man called twice a week to take them to be recharged. In 1937 we purchased a modern radio, and as at this time our house only had gas this set was battery operated. The large council estate that we lived on did not get electricity until the mid 1950s.'

One of the first radios in Hayes in the 1930s; this was before they were enclosed in cabinets!

⬚ SOUTHALL CINEMAS ⬚

'There used to be four cinemas – the Odeon, the Palace, the Dominion and the Gem. The Odeon was in the High Street opposite the White Hart. The Palace was in South Road, just around the corner, built in the style of a Chinese building; it was later renamed the Gaumont. A bomb fell next to it during the war, demolishing a shop but the cinema still stood. The Dominion was south of the railway line, on the ABC circuit. I believe it was opened in 1937 by Gracie Fields. The Odeon had a pre-war Saturday morning Mickey Mouse Club for children. I used to get in for threepence.'

'Each Saturday before the war we went to the pictures at the Odeon cinema, Southall, big rival to the Palace down South Road. There were competitions each week, such as "Cleanest pair of shoes" and "Biggest list of road signs". The cinema had an organ and we sang the following song with gusto:

> "We come along on Saturday morning,
> Greeting everybody with a smile,
> We come along on Saturday morning,
> Knowing it is all worthwhile.
>
> As members of the Odeon Club,
> We all intend to be
> Good citizens when we grow up
> And champions of the free.
>
> We come along on Saturday morning,
> Greeting everybody with a smile, smile, smile,
> Greeting everybody with a smile."

I can remember the tune perfectly well. Unfortunately, I am no musician so cannot write the swingy rhythm of the tune down. Fortunately you cannot hear my singing either!'

The boating lake at Southall Park before the war.

⊠ UXBRIDGE 'FLICKS' ⊠

'When I came to Uxbridge in 1953, Coronation year, the town had three cinemas – the Savoy, the Odeon, and the Regal. Having a television was a luxury and most of us looked forward to an evening at the "flicks".

In those days you were allowed in during a performance. Usually we had to queue outside until the doorman allowed us in as seats became available. Once inside we were guided by a uniformed usherette to where we were to sit.

Sometimes the adverts would be on, or the Pathe News, the trailer for next week's show, or maybe a cartoon. If we were unlucky, it would be the end of the supporting film, or the last minutes of the feature film. It would be like looking at the end of a book before reading it and we would know how the story would end.

Best of all would be to come during the interval when the lights were up and the organist would be playing. The only queue would be for ice cream bought from a poor girl standing to the side of the front row. The weight of the loaded tray harnessed around her neck made her round shouldered, but it left her hands free to serve ices or drinks and to take the money almost at the same time.

What a difference nowadays! With the onset of television the Savoy, having outlived its popularity, became a bingo hall before being demolished. The Regal was converted into a night club, being saved from destruction by a preservation order on the art deco facade. There is also a preservation order on the Compton organ inside. The Odeon is the only remaining cinema, but the original building was also destroyed before being rebuilt as a modern two-screen cinema.'

▩ TOTTENHAM MEMORIES ▩

'Tottenham has long been associated with the Spurs – one of the glamour football teams. During the early 1950s my father took me with him to home matches, and for some strange reason one of the players from that time is imprinted in my memory – Alf Ramsey, who many years later became manager of the England side. I can still see the men playing in shorts way past their knees and heavy laced boots which seemed nearly to meet the shorts.

The other entertainment high spot was the Royal – a dance hall where Dave Clarke's Five played, "The Creep" was introduced to dance halls, and many top bands starred.

Our other entertainment centres were the Finsbury Park Empire – we went there most Saturdays and saw most of the top stars of variety, including Max Miller who made us children wonder why adults laughed so much at him – and the Finsbury Park Astoria, a wonderful 1930s cinema decorated as a Moorish palace where one could have tea served by "Nippies" in black dresses and snowy-white aprons and caps.'

ROYAL DAYS

We all shared in royal occasions, the happy and the sad. Towns and villages all over Middlesex celebrated jubilees and coronations, and mourned the passing of the King.

▣ MEDALS AND MUGS ▣
'To celebrate the Silver Jubilee of George V in 1935, all the children at our school in Willesden were given a medal and a tuckbox of food. From the front of our house we could see the LMS railway line and often saw the old King and Queen Mary waving from a carriage window as they travelled to and from London. Then for the Coronation of George VI in 1937 we were given a commemorative mug.'

▣ FUNERAL AND CORONATION ▣
'It was a cold morning in February 1952. As I worked for British Rail at Paddington station I was allowed, with the rest of the staff, to line the exit road as the funeral procession of George VI passed down to Platform 8 where the special Royal train was waiting to carry the coffin to Windsor. As the gun carriage passed the spot where I stood all that could be heard was the sound of the wheels on the cobbled stones and the marching feet, everything else was dead quiet.

Later that day my father, who had also worked for British Rail at Hayes station told me that, as the train slowly passed through the station, all the local staff dressed in their best uniforms, including caps, and all the local dignitaries were lining the down main platform standing to attention and saluting as the train passed. Also Hayes bridge was packed with people waiting to pay their last respects to a great man. At the local factories, which bordered the railway line, their staff were also out waiting. People waited quietly in the fields and roads nearby. I heard later that this was echoed at all the stations, Southall, West Drayton, Iver and Slough, and all along the line to Windsor. It was a day that will live in people's memories for a very long time.

For the Queen's coronation, 2nd June 1953 was declared a day's holiday, and as it would be very crowded in London and almost impossible to see anything, it was decided by all the people in our street, Birchway, that those who had televisions, which were still very expensive, would invite neighbours into their homes to watch it. I remember that I had arranged to go into our next door neighbour's house. We congregated there just before it was due to start and all went well until the Princess arrived at the Abbey then – wham – the screen went blank. There was nothing we could do, so everyone upped and ran across the road, adults and children, to my sister-in-law's father's house where the next television was. There was no time to bother to find chairs so we just sat on the floor in front of the people who were already there and watched the whole programme, which lasted for several hours. The visiting ladies took plates of sandwiches and cakes with them for a "pot luck" snack. The television was in black and white but this did not detract from the splendour of the occasion. Everyone had a wonderful day and the neighbourly feeling in those days was something to be cherished.'

▣ ALL STAND ▣

'On the day of the Queen's coronation in 1953 whole families stayed riveted to the television screen and marvelled at the scene set before them. Our family was very loyal and we all stood up in front of the screen when the National Anthem played for the last time that day.'

ALL THROUGH THE YEAR

Every year brought its regular days of celebration and fun, from fairs and carnivals to cricket matches, Ascot and the Boat Race.

◉ BOAT RACE DAY ◉

'Each year in the 1930s there was great excitement and rivalry as the day approached of the Oxford and Cambridge University Boat Race. We each had to support either Oxford or Cambridge and wear a favour to declare our allegiance. These favours were usually made of dark blue or light blue celluloid in the form of a rosette and we purchased them at the local sweetshop. Children who had a lot of pocket money often wore a little celluloid doll dressed in the colour of their "side" and with a big furry hat on its head. Even to this day I am still "Cambridge", mainly because my brothers were "Oxford".'

◉ EASTER SUNDAY ◉

'As a child I always looked forward to Easter, not just because I knew I would be getting several Easter eggs but because I would be getting a new set of Sunday Best clothes.

My mother was a member of the Co-op and she used to put so much away each week on vouchers so that we children always had good clothes. As soon as she had paid for one lot she would start another. Easter was always special.

A few weeks previously my mother and I would have gone along to one of the large Co-op stores at either Southall, Hounslow or Hammersmith and bought me a new dress, coat, matching straw hat with flowers on it, socks, new shoes and, of course, white gloves. After showing these off to my father and older brothers, who, by this time were going to work so clothed themselves, all the clothes were put away until Easter Sunday.

How proud I was on Easter Sunday morning walking to Sunday school all decked out in my new clothes, I felt as if I really was strutting along on the Easter Parade.

When I eventually went out to work every week my father made me put ten shillings away in Co-op vouchers so that every 20 weeks, roughly spring, autumn and Christmas, I always had £10 out, enough to by myself a new rig-out. He always maintained that if I worked in an office I should have nice clothes to go to work in. It seemed hard at first when I only had low wages, but I thanked him afterwards when I saw that my friends never seemed to have enough money to buy clothes to wear when going anywhere special.'

▨ May Queen ▨

'They chose me. Primarily because I had long fair hair, but the reason didn't matter. The fact was, they chose me – I was to be the May Queen.

All the other girls had bridesmaids' dresses to wear, but I had never been a bridesmaid, so I had to borrow Jacqueline's. It was bright pink. They untied my long fair plaits (an act for which I was sorely scolded on returning home), and dressed my hair with May blossom, buttercups and clover. I felt absolutely wonderful!

It was just after the war, and we all lived in "pre-fabs" with long gardens full of early summer flowers and vegetables. At the back of the pre-fabs ran Willow Tree Lane, which led into open fields of clover, flanked with bursting hedgerows. But the lane wasn't public enough for our procession.

We found an old roadsweeper's handcart, temporarily abandoned at the end of the lane, threw out the old brooms, and put me in their place. It was filthy inside, but it served the purpose precisely, and I was paraded up and down Ruislip Road for all to see. We felt so important and even received the odd beep from the few motor cars which passed by.

We ended our journey at the buttercup field where we danced

Maypole dancing on the green at West Drayton in the 1920s.

round an imaginary maypole waving brightly coloured hair ribbons in our hands.

These were the days of innocent hope for the future, when the early summer air was heavy with the scent of blossom and fields really were golden with buttercups. There's a housing estate on the buttercup field now.'

◈ Off to Ascot ◈

'The horse and cart which was used for delivering sausages in Twickenham was also used for pleasurable day's outings to Ascot races. Early in the morning on a Bank Holiday the cart was loaded up with baskets of food, crates of drink, and all the family would get aboard and off they would set. On arriving at steep hills, such as Egham Hill, everyone except the driver would get off and walk and some would push the cart to help the poor old horse up the hill. On arrival at Ascot the cart was unloaded, the horse watered and fed. A relaxed and happy day was spent by one and all. The ladies chatted, children played and the men had a bob or two on the horses – win or lose they did not mind. All returned home, tired and happy having enjoyed the day's outing which was the highlight of the year.'

◈ The Summer Cricket Match ◈

'I remember as a child in the 1930s that every year in the summer two of the local public houses at Norwood Green, the Lamb and the Wolf, would play an annual cricket match against each other. The prize was a large cricket bat which stood about eight to ten feet tall. Each year it was inscribed with the name of the winning team and stood outside their pub until it was defended the following year.

This was a great day out for the whole village, families would take picnics with them to eat on the green and children would play games on the outskirts of the field.

I remember that on one corner of the green was a large structure made of iron shaped like a crown, open at the top with two crossover arches. I always wondered what it was until one day my father took me inside and I found out that it was a "gentleman's privy".

These annual tournaments continued, except for the war years, up until about 15 years ago when other teams wanted to be included, but unfortunately they didn't want to do the work involved in preparing the field, etc so it was abandoned. The last time I saw the "bat" it was still outside the Wolf public house.'

◼ FROM BRASS BAND TO HURDY GURDY ◼

'Before the Second World War the Hayes and Harlington Silver Band was one of the most well known bands in the country. They entered all the big brass band competitions and won many cups. They also held one of the biggest outdoor competitions, which included marching. Unfortunately this had to be abandoned during the war although the band still continued on.

I remember one evening in the early part of the war my two brothers coming home with instruments; they had joined the Silver Band. Jack had a trombone and Henry a cornet. They were both trained musicians having learnt with the Salvation Army during their younger days. Their friend George, who could not play a note, had a big bass and my brothers were going to teach him to play. As my mother was in the kitchen cooking chips for supper, the boys were in the lounge teaching George the basic scales when suddenly the siren sounded and a string of bombs dropped along the bottom end of the road where we lived, Birchway, and Hunters Grove, damaging several houses. George decided then that the bass was not for him and he took it back at the next practice night. My brothers remained with the band until they were eventually called up to serve in the Forces. I remember how proud I was, as a young girl of ten or eleven, following the band when it marched through Hayes Town, Jack in the front line and Henry at the back. They were both much older than I was.

After the war the band tried to revive the Open Air Brass Band Competition in Hayes and had a very successful day in Hayes

Park in the late 1940s. The silver cups used as prizes were taken from the bank where they had been stored for safety and cleaned. Bands came from all over the country, it was an all-day event and once again each band had to march as they were playing. What a sight, it was a lovely July day, the instruments were gleaming in the sun, and the gold braiding and brass buttons on the immaculate uniforms also shone.

When the band applied to hire the park from the park authorities the next year they could only have it if the authority were also allowed to participate in the event by hiring out stalls to local charities, etc. This was agreed and, once again, it was a successful day. The following year the park authorities took it over completely, which proved to be the death of the band competition because the bands did not fancy having to compete against the music coming from the hurdy-gurdy of a fun fair. This event was the forerunner of the Hayes Town Fete which is still held every summer. The band still continued, even successfully winning the first prize in their section of the Star Band Competition at the Albert Hall. The conductor, Mr Green, was so excited that when he telephoned his wife to tell her the news he couldn't speak and I had to tell her for him. Eventually the band was renamed the Hillingdon Borough Band, and I believe it is still in existence today.'

◙ WEALDSTONE'S SUMMER PROCESSION ◙
'Once a year in the 1930s there was a Summer Procession through Wealdstone. Local firms and societies supported floats, and gaily dressed clowns carried buckets for sightseers' pennies. This was to support the Harrow Hospital in West Street, before the National Health Service was introduced.'

◙ ASHFORD HORTICULTURAL SHOW ◙
'A great occasion at the time of the First World War was Ashford Horticultural Society Show, which took place on Farmer Cook's fields. A row of marquees was erected to house the displays of flowers, fruit and vegetables. There were classes for cottagers and professional gardeners, flower arranging, various crafts and cooking and displays from the Industrial School children. There were competitions for the amateur fire brigade, bonny babies, the best legs, and to climb the greasy pole! The band played and there were fireworks and dancing, swings and roundabouts and we had a half day holiday from school. What a great day.'

◙ A SMALL ROUNDABOUT ◙
'When I was a child living in Harlesden in the late 1920s, at certain times of the year a small roundabout would appear around the corner from where I lived in St John's Avenue, and if we took jam jars we could have a free ride, exciting to us children in those days.'

◙ STANWELL FAIR ◙
'In the Middle Ages many charters were given to towns and

Stanwell Fair earlier in the century.

villages to hold fairs. Unfortunately, not too many have survived. The village of Stanwell still has theirs. This is on 26th May, St Augustine's Day.

When I was a small girl in Stanwell, like others, after Christmas pennies were saved for the fair. The magic of the caravans appearing from nowhere, so to speak, was wonderful to children, with the colourful people of the fair, and their chickens transported underneath! At six o'clock the night before, the village policeman blew a whistle and the fairmen in a line rushed to get the best site.

A special sweet was sold called "Stanwell Rock". The makers at the fair threw the pliable mixture up and around hooks. Very fascinating to watch. I remember boxing booths where local boys challenged the fair boxer. My mother remembers the fair when horses were sold and my great grandfather told me how "hiring"

Halliford Bend and Shepperton Lock between the wars, popular spots on bank holidays and weekends.

used to take place at the fair where a farm labourer could stand with a pitchfork, or a domestic maid with a mop, etc, to be sold and given life and soul to their employer.

Boys from the local school used to play truant to watch the fair pack up, knowing full well the day after they would suffer a good caning back at school. However, they thought it worth it!'

◈ ICKENHAM FAIR ◈

'Until the Second World War a fair was held annually about Whitsuntide in the centre of the village. The roundabout, the greatest attraction, always stood in the forecourt of the Coach and Horses. Under the terms of the charter, Ickenham fair would only continue to be held as long as one stallholder attended on the official day. One year Hillingdon fair attracted all the gypsies and none came to Ickenham. Everyone was disappointed, especially the children who drifted home, but a hoop-la stall was rushed down to Ickenham and although it did very little business the right had been preserved. In 1936 no stalls arrived in Ickenham on fair day so the right to hold a fair was lost for ever.'

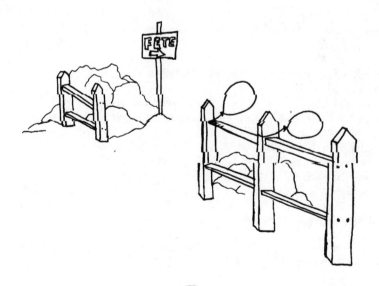

INDEX

223

LIST OF CONTRIBUTING INSTITUTES

Contributions have been received from the following Middlesex Women's Institutes:

Alperton & Wembley ● Ashford ● Ashford Afternoon
Chiswick Clay Hill ● Cowley ● Ealing ● Eastbury ● Eastcote
Field End ● Forty Hill ● Grange Park Afternoon ● Grange Park
Evening Greenfielde ● Greenford Evening ● Halliford
Harlington ● Hayes Town ● Hillingdon ● Hillingdon Village
Ickenham ● Ickenham Village Afternoon ● Iver Evening
Laleham Evening Laleham Village ● Lea Valley ● Manor Farm
Northolt Afternoon ● Norwood Green ● North Hillingdon
Afternoon ● Pinner ● Ruislip Common ● Shepperton Green
Shepperton Village ● Southbourne ● South Eastcote ● Stanmore
Stanwell ● Sudbury ● Sunbury-on-Thames ● Twickenham
Uxbridge Afternoon ● West Drayton ● Yeading.